Virtual Caliphate

Related Titles from Potomac Books, Inc.

Terror on the Internet: The New Arena, the New Challenges
—Gabriel Weimann

Human Intelligence, Counterterrorism, and National Leadership: A Practical Guide
—Gary Berntsen

Al-Qa'ida's Doctrine for Insurgency: Abd al-Aziz al-Muqrin's "A Practical Course for Guerrilla War"
—Translated and Analyzed by Norman Cigar

Ideas as Weapons: Influence and Perception in Modern Warfare
—G. J. David, Jr., and T. R. McKeldin III, eds.

The Path to Paradise: The Inner World of Suicide Bombers and Their Dispatchers
—Anat Berko

Breeding Ground: Afghanistan and the Origins of Islamist Terrorism
—Deepak Tripathi

The Banality of Suicide Terrorism: The Naked Truth About the Psychology of Islamic Suicide Bombing
—Nancy Hartevelt Kobrin

Virtual Caliphate

Exposing the Islamist State on the Internet

YAAKOV LAPPIN

Potomac Books, Inc.
Washington, D.C.

Library of Congress Cataloging-in-Publication Data
Lappin, Yaakov.
Virtual caliphate : exposing the Islamist state on the internet / Yaakov Lappin. — 1st ed.
p. cm.
Includes bibliographical references and index.
ISBN 978-1-59797-511-7 (hardcover : alk. paper)
1. Terrorism—Computer network resources. 2. Terrorism—Prevention. 3. Islam—Computer network resources. 4. Islamic fundamentalism. I. Title.
HV6431.L3465 2010
363.3250285'4678—dc22
2010035149

Printed in the United States of America on acid-free paper that meets the American National Standards Institute Z39-48 Standard.

Potomac Books, Inc.
22841 Quicksilver Drive
Dulles, Virginia 20166

First Edition

10 9 8 7 6 5 4 3 2 1

Contents

Introduction

Since the attacks of September 11, 2001, the world has scrambled to understand the force that brought down the Twin Towers in New York and struck the Pentagon in Washington. The same force has since continued to wreck death and destruction around the globe. Despite being significantly damaged after the attacks, the jihadi movement continues to embark on holy war day and night, striking targets in dozens of states. Recruiting thousands of volunteers ready to sacrifice themselves, it acts in the full belief that it is carrying out God's will.

This movement interprets the writings of a seventh-century religious prophet and political leader as direct orders from a commander in chief. It tags fellow coreligionists who hold different interpretations of Islam as the foremost enemy.

Because the mind-set of the jihadi movement is so fundamentally alien to that of the West, decision makers, the media, and others have at times failed to understand what makes jihadis tick. Catch phrases such as "the war on terror" only contribute to the confusion by focusing on the tactics of jihadis, not on the jihadis themselves.

The same fog surrounds the jihadis' use of the Internet. Although the fact that the Internet is used in some way by al Qaeda is well known, the media spotlight often shines on specific uses of the web by jihadis. One report will focus on how al Qaeda members used the Internet to carry out a terrorist attack, while another will quote a speech by a jihadi leader made available on the Internet. These, however, are snippets of a much larger phenomenon.

In order to grasp the full picture, it is best to take a step back and adopt a bird's eye view of the tremendous amount of online jihadi activity taking place at this very moment. This world is merely a few clicks away from any web surfer.

One could argue that, from a certain angle, when staring at the bottomless pit that is online jihadi activity, a structure can be discerned. Could the structure be a new and revolutionary way that members of a movement organize themselves? Is it possible to claim that an online state has been formed for the purpose of eventually creating a geographical state?

The caliphate is the name of the Islamic state begun by Islam's prophet, Muhammad. It was dismantled with the demise of the Ottoman Empire, which was the last caliphate in history. Today, countless websites are dedicated to its reestablishment. Virtual clerics preach jihad in order to make that state real. Online training camps have been formed to teach soldiers how to make bombs or fire a rocket. Online planners are mapping out the state's tax laws and constitution.

This book is an attempt to clear the mist surrounding online jihadi activities and to suggest that radical Islam and a large portion of what is known as al Qaeda are hovering in cyberspace.

One could argue that "ministries" of war, morality, foreign affairs, and finance can all be discerned within a developing virtual caliphate.

In the meantime, this virtual caliphate—if it exists—continues to confound. The first step is to try and answer a basic question: are online jihadis organized?

1
The Strangers

"Without a doubt, the Internet is the single most important venue for the radicalization of Islamic youth."

—*U.S. Army Brig. Gen. John Custer, head of intelligence at Central Command*[1]

In the mid-1990s, Osama Bin Laden stood in a dark cave, hidden away in the wild mountains of Afghanistan. The soon-to-be world's most wanted man was holding a press interview with Abdel Bari Atwan, a Palestinian editor in chief of a London-based pan-Arab newspaper.[2] Atwan is the one of the few journalists who gained access to Bin Laden when the latter was in the midst of planning the 9/11 attacks. Even though the meeting took place in the late 1990s, Bin Laden already exhibited a heightened awareness of the changing nature of global communications, and the vital role that the Internet was destined to play in the future of his movement."The ummah [global Islamic community] is connected like an electric current," Bin Laden told Atwan during the interview. Reflecting on this encounter with Bin Laden in his book *The Secret History of al-Qaida,* Atwan wrote that he had made a striking observation. "I discovered that, in contrast with the primitive accommodation, the base was well equipped with computers and up-to-the-minute communications equipment. Bin Laden had access to the internet, which was not then ubiquitous as it is now, and said: 'These days the world is becoming like a small village.' . . . One of his aides laughed and said the base was 'a republic within a republic.'"

More than ten years ago, al Qaeda planted the seeds of a phenomenon that can be called the virtual caliphate—an Islamic state that exists on the Internet. Bin Laden realized early on that the Internet offered international terrorist organizations the opportunity for their members to keep in touch with one another. He probably did not intend to create anything resembling a virtual caliphate. In fact, the concept of an online state sounds much like a fantasy. But a number of historical developments, such as the rapid development of electronic communications and the loss of al-Qaeda's only territorial safe zone in Afghanistan, have caused its creation. Although this virtual entity has not yet been described by security commentators, journalists, and other opinion makers as a "state," there is cause to argue that jihadi websites function together much like the organs of an independent political-religious entity.

The virtual caliphate is made up of thousands of interconnected computers, chat rooms, and servers on the Internet, which are held together by a common purpose. The multitudes of online jihadis use cutting edge technology to plot terrorist attacks and share blueprints for the caliphate. Al Qaeda may well have succeeded in creating a virtual version of its former base in Afghanistan's maze of caves.

A decade after Bin Laden's interview with Atwan and thousands of miles away, an Islamist preacher in London used a jihadi chat room to incite dozens of listeners to violence.

This type of chat room truly gives the feel of being in a physical room with others. Users can not only exchange text messages over the Internet but can also speak and hear one another by using microphones.

The room was filled with young, excited, mostly British, Muslims. The cause of the excitement was a live talk being given by their leader, Sheikh Omar Bakri. He was talking about just one thing that night: holy war.

"I am speaking about the UK. Why it became Dar al-Harb [a land of war]," Bakri told his online followers.[3] Their names were listed on the right-hand side of the screen to indicate their presence. Bakri had a full room. Although the Syrian-born cleric has a thick Arabic accent, he spoke fluently in English that night. With a lively, hoarse voice, he employed it for a single and very serious purpose—to call on his listeners to kill.

"I believe the whole of Britain has become Dar al-Harb," Bakri said, using a watchword that plays a key role in modern jihadi ideology.[4] Centuries ago, Islamic scholars ruled that the world is divided into the *Dar al-Islam* (House of Islam) and the *Dar al-Harb* (Land of War), the areas of the world not yet under Islamic law. One of the aims of jihad is to bring the land of war under the control of the House of Islam. The problem, jihadis say, is that the House of Islam does not exist today. According to Bakri, the only place that qualifies as Dar al-Islam—a true house of Islam—was his own chat room, along with any other site on the Internet that matched his fervent desire to found the caliphate.

The United Kingdom must "really start [the war]," Bakri continued, because British authorities "arrest religious Muslim scholars . . . they declare your job is to divide the Muslims, [to] promote secularism, [and] integration . . . This is what makes [the UK] Dar al-Harb."[5]

The sermon lasted for hours and was followed by an interactive question-and-answer session. Bakri spoke about a "victorious group," who, like Islam's founder and first ruler of the Islamic state, Muhammad, would create a caliphate—a state governed according to the rules of the Koran—after destroying the world's current impure regimes.

"We have lost the caliphate in 1924 but continue the victorious group into today. We have Sheikh Osama bin Laden, our leader, and he is admired by every single person, so that is the victorious group," declared Bakri.[6]

"Al Qaeda and all its branches and organisations of the world, that is the victorious group, and they have the emir, and you are obliged to join," Bakri told an eager audience.[7]

"If you want to be killed, you've got to have fire. Fight until Allah's *deen* [law] is dominant or until you become a *shaheed* [martyr]. I'm sure you get the message," Bakri said. One user in the chat room typed "YES" on the screen in response. Somewhere, a person was resonating with this call for jihad.[8]

A woman then asked Bakri whether she needed permission from her husband to become a suicide bomber. Bakri told the woman she needed no such permission and cited religious and historical precedents to drive home the point that in a time of war women could carry out an act of jihad without their husbands' approval.

Another user typed in the chat box: "Do you believe that the flag of *shahada* [martyrdom] should fly over 10 Downing St [home of the British prime minister and cabinet]?" In other words, should the seat of the British government be bombed? Other followers took turns using the room's microphone to ask questions. All of those who spoke had British accents. The formation of a possible UK terrorist cell was being played out on my computer screen.

Six months after Bakri declared Britain to be a legitimate target for a jihad attack in 2005, four British-born suicide bombers blew themselves up in London, murdering fifty-two people, in Britain's worst-ever terrorist attack. Were those suicide bombers in the chat room at the time? Evidence suggests that they were in touch with the online cleric, Omar Bakri, and used the Internet to organize much of their attack. Police and the government attempted to figure out how four British men became radicalized to the point of committing mass murder against their fellow citizens. As the hunt for answers was underway, the Paltalk chat room calling on UK Muslims to become martyrs continued to be open on a nightly basis.

Bakri returned to the same chat room many times since delivering that sermon, and his haunting recruitment calls remained as dangerous as ever. "I don't want you to join me, I want you to join these people . . . Allah said these are the victorious. And today the leader of that victorious . . . is well-known leader of the camp of jihad, Osama bin Laden. Therefore support him. Be with them."[9] Speaking of dead terrorists, Bakri called out from my computer speakers: "'These people are calling you and shouting to you from far distant places: al jihad, al jihad. They say to you my dear Muslim brothers, 'Where is your weapon, where is your weapon?' Come on to the jihad.'"[10]

After the London bombings, Bakri, afraid of being arrested, left the United Kingdom for Lebanon and was refused reentry by the British authorities. But the Internet easily bridged the physical barrier separating the online jihadi preacher and his dedicated followers, and several of his audio sermons and messages continued to make their way to Britain over the Internet.[11]

Searching for a Home

The siren calls of the entity that I have labeled as the virtual caliphate reel in radicalized Muslims from around the world, with the promise of an ideal and pure Islamic state, and the message of hatred for existing civilizations.

The virtual caliphate is founded on a complete rejection of the current world order. Established by Islamist jihadi organizations, it is driven by the belief that the nations of the world are not being ruled as they should be, according to a strict interpretation of Islamic law.

By no means, however, are the jihadis' voices the only Muslim voices heard on the Internet. The presence of moderate Islamic preachers has been felt online, although that presence has so far been less ferocious and less successful than the jihadis' in utilizing the Internet to gain and mobilize followers.

This difference is primarily because, unlike moderate Muslim leaders, proponents of global jihadism do not usually control their own mosques, nor do they enjoy state-supported resources. For jihadis, the Internet is the substitute for all that they lack in the physical world.

One example of an alternative and moderate Islamic online phenomenon is the Sufi Internet presence. Sufis take a mystical approach to Islam and place an emphasis on internal spiritual processes. Sufi websites focus on "inner struggles," as outlined in the thousand-year-old writings of Sufi philosopher Abu Hamid Muhammad al-Ghazali.[12]

Instead of feverish discussions on establishing the caliphate and dealing with infidels, Sufi websites offer advice on how to limit one's ego and suggest cures for depression.[13]

But jihadis use the virtual caliphate to call for sweeping, apocalyptic destruction and for the replacement of the current world order with a global, physical Islamist state. They derive their zeal and confidence, as well as their thirst for mass murder, from an unswerving belief that they are acting on a divine mandate. Jihadis use the Internet to instill that same brainwashing in the minds of others. In fact, the topic of Sufi Islam is regularly raised in jihadi forums as a target for scorn and contempt. It is trivialized as a counterfeit form of Islam.

The organizers of the international jihad face a serious predicament. On the one hand, they wish to raise an army, form their own state, expand its borders, and govern the planet. On the other hand, they have failed to establish full control of any territory at this time. How can an international movement with global aspirations survive while it is stateless and being hunted down by a powerful coalition of countries it has attacked? How can it maintain a war while having no base from which to organize its operations?

Jihadis actually have no place to call home. They consider Arab and Muslim countries such as Egypt, Jordan, Saudi Arabia, and Pakistan to be treacherous puppets of Western anti-Islamic forces that dominate the world. Unsurprisingly, Islamists have been severely repressed by the Arab regimes and states they so despise. Al Qaeda–affiliated websites will often issue a call to kill a leader of a Muslim state, as in July 2008 when Abu Yahya al-Libi posted a video on a jihadi website.

King Abdullah of Saudi Arabia had provoked al-Libi's wrath because he held an interfaith dialogue conference on Saudi soil. King Abdullah's invitation to Christians and Jews to partake in the dialogue conference provoked the fury of jihadis everywhere. "'Hurrying to kill this wanton tyrant (King Abdullah) who has announced himself to be a leader of atheism would be among the most pious acts,'" al-Libi declared in the video.[14]

The war between jihadi movements and Arab-Muslim states has been raging for decades. Muslim countries (the term "Muslim" to describe those states would be disputed by Islamists) are the most hostile environments for Islamists to operate in—a fact that helped prompt an exile of jihadis in the 1980s and '90s from the Middle East to the safer shores of the West. Many washed up in Western Europe, especially Britain, while others sought refuge elsewhere.

The failure of the jihadis to rise to power in the Muslim world, as they wished to do, was one of the key factors that drove them to strike the United States on September 11, 2001. Al Qaeda had hoped to harness the military power of the world's sole superpower in order to destabilize and bring down the Arab-Muslim governments they sought to replace. The idea is to clear the path for the reestablishment of a caliphate, which means attacking the Asian-Arab states currently standing in its way. The success or failure of this shift in strategy is being decided now in battlegrounds around the world, in Iraq, in Afghanistan, and other lower-profile arenas.

Irrespective of how they choose to go about it, the jihadis have not swerved from their most important and basic goal of rebuilding the Islamic state, the caliphate.

So long as this goal is not reached, Islamists will continue to rely on the Internet, because it is the only place their state will not be destroyed.

What would a virtual state look like? Who "resides" in it? And what are its aims?

Jihadis have set up shop on the Internet in order to temporarily keep their movement as cohesive as possible. At a later stage, jihadis hope to use their web presence as a launching pad for an attempted coup to overthrow Asian-Arab-Muslim governments; to replace these with a caliphate state; and ultimately, as fanciful as it sounds, to conquer the planet.

An online Islamist state seeking an "upload" into the real world would need an army to achieve this goal. The question of whether a virtual caliphate exists remains open, but what is beyond dispute is that a number of Muslim youths are being recruited into the ranks of the *mujahadeen* (holy warriors) online.

Raising an army via the Internet is perhaps the most important task of the online jihadi presence. It is a task that is impossible to carry out without some very effective online brainwashing. Unfortunately, the Internet provides an excellent means to indoctrinate people.

Becoming a Stranger

To watch recruitment propaganda for the jihadi army is a chilling experience. A huge number of websites provide videos, recorded sermons, and downloadable books, all of which are aimed at enlisting Muslims for the global jihad.

The implications of this phenomenon are enormous. No matter how moderate the local mosque, Muslim youths will still be at risk and targeted for indoctrination through the Internet.

If successful, these messages will suck their audience into the worldwide network of holy fighters. The virtual caliphate can in effect come out from behind the screen and grab its audience, sending them to fight anywhere thanks to its borderless form and instant ability to transmit messages and orders. Whether the target zone is a local city center or a conflict area thousands of miles away, the online jihadi presence has already created soldiers and dispatched them to battlegrounds.

A British Islamic website, al-Ghurabaa, which is no longer accessible, was formed by followers of Omar Bakri, the online jihadi preacher exiled to Lebanon. The website encouraged users to download recruitment videos. These messages need to be examined in order to understand how jihadis enlist others to join their cause.

In one video, a digital image of a desert pans across the computer screen, and men can be heard chanting a single word in the background like a mantra, *Ghurabaa, Ghurabaa* [the strangers, the strangers].[15]

The first Muslims, according to the video, were perceived as strangers by the non-Muslims of their time. The word "strangers" is used here as a positive term. It describes individuals who have successfully accessed God's message. The newly enlightened Muslims appear strange to the remainder of the populace, stuck in an age of ignorance.

"Be with Ghurabaa, be with the strangers"[16] large white letters instructs the viewer, as the repeated chanting continues. "The prophet Muhammad said, Islam came as something strange . . . And it will return as something strange,"[17] the message declares triumphantly, showing an image of hundreds of thousands of people bowed in Islamic prayer form at a Meccan mosque.

These strangers are assured paradise, the video promises. A triumph for Islam in this world or heaven in the next are the two visions held in the minds of brainwashed mujahadeen, and these goals are visually depicted in this video, alongside verses from the Koran being chanted. The overall effect is powerful.

Quoting the Koran, the video tells viewers that "the strangers" of Muhammad's time were "those who withdrew from their people, and their disbelief, customs, and traditions . . . Those who forbid the evil when the people become corrupted.'"[18]

Withdrawal from society is a key message. Without that disengagement from the "evildoers" all around, one cannot tap into the holy power of Allah, the video insists. Inevitably, for anyone who accepts this message, the people around them will begin to appear lowly, ignorant, and eventually as the enemy.

The strangers fled to the cave, says the video, to escape "those who do wrong" and "ones who lie against Allah."[19] Like Osama Bin Laden's cave, packed with computers and al Qaeda members accessing the Internet, this online video uses the latest technology to urge Muslims to retreat from their "sinful" societies, rebel against modernism, and rebuild their identities in order to become jihadis.

The message's aim is to alienate young Muslims and dislodge them from their societies. This is achieved by implanting the message into their minds that their environments are morally corrupt and that the world order must be destroyed. Such a message can be delivered safely on the Internet.

But why are new jihadi recruits wholeheartedly accepting it? According to Olivier Roy, author of *Globalized Islam*, some second-generation Muslim youths born into minority communities in the West feel cut off from the cultures of their old countries and seek to reconstruct their identities by embracing a puritanical form of Islam. If Roy is correct, the visitors to the English-language websites that distribute such videos are being targeted for identity restructuring. Your old identity is based on a lie, they are told. "For many neo-fundamentalists, globalization is an opportunity, not a loss," writes Roy.

Not preached in moderate mosques

In fact, Roy believes that the very effort to reestablish the caliphate is an expression of weakness by the jihadis, as they base their idolized state on a historical model that is largely myth. Further, the desire for a new self-definition is in and of itself a "by-product of globalization," he argues.

The caliphate most certainly did exist in many forms throughout the centuries, though clearly it was not the idyllic kingdom its modern advocates believe it to be. Roy helps explain why the jihadi Internet message is being so loudly and clearly received in the West. In Arab-Asian-Muslim states, other factors, such as regime oppression and a lack of freedom of speech, could be ripening youths for a radical alternative and leading them into the arms of jihadi ideologues.

The attempt to alienate new recruits, whether they reside in Western states as minority citizens or in Arab-Muslim countries as part of the majority population, is aimed at cutting them off from what jihadis see as the polluting and backward ungodly forces that currently rule the world.

The video is peppered with quotes from the Koran and the *hadith* (oral traditions), which are selectively used to back up the message that the time has come to distance one's self from society. With no qualified Islamic scholar to explain the contexts of the quotes, the targeted viewer is left thinking that Islam sanctions this viewpoint.

Viewers are urged to "turn away" from the sinful people, and in return God will "shower his mercy" upon them.[20] Muslims are also urged to turn their backs on their families if their loved ones fail to accept the jihadi path.

The video establishes two paths: the "good" path as ordered by Allah, jihad, Islam, and the establishment of the caliphate on the one hand; and the "evil" path on the other that represents all people, systems, or beliefs that contradict this worldview.

A voice on the video sings out Koranic verses in oriental Middle Eastern style—all part of the effort to stamp this message with a religious seal of approval.

The call to retreat from society is now, jihadis hope, firmly entrenched in the viewer's mind, as the video turns to galvanizing its audience toward the next inevitable stage: warfare.

In the second half of the video, Osama Bin Laden and al Qaeda are presented as contemporary versions of Muhammad and his companions, a parallel that is both shocking and dangerous.

"The prophet and his companions made *hijrah* [migrated] and fought jihad for the sake of Allah, they left all their worldly affairs for the jihad," explains the white text, which now flashes on and off rapidly against an image of a masked mujahadeen armed with a machine gun.[21]

"Be with the ghurabaa, be with the strangers," the video urges. "Be like them and follow them as Allah ordered."[22]

The video then asks its viewers to identify today's righteous stranger. The answer could not be clearer, as the letters forming the question fade into an image of one burning Trade Tower and then the image of the other tower absorbing the impact of the second plane in the September 11 terrorist attack.

This is how jihadis use a successful terrorist attack to try and recruit more people to repeat the act.

Without warning, the chanting suddenly assumes a fast, militaristic tone and tempo, as sounds of machine guns being fired can be heard in the background. Images of men training with weapons, hostages in Iraq (who are later decapitated), and various bombings, shootings, and other acts of jihad are shown in a dizzyingly fast visual procession.

Al Qaeda members are the strangers of today, the contemporary equivalents of Muhammad and his companions and the upholders of a divine way, the video tells its audience. Just as Muhammad and his companions were perceived as being "strange," so too is al Qaeda by the sinful world of today, the message says. Still photographs of Osama Bin Laden pepper the video, as well as images of his deputy, Ayman al-Zawahiri.

The video now reaches its peak. "O Muslims, be with the terrorists! Do not be with the *kuffar* [infidels]! The *kuffar* will never be pleased with you until you follow their *deen* [law]! Be with the Muslims! O Allah give the victory to the *mujahadeen.* O Allah! Destroy America. O Allah! Destroy the enemies of Islam and Muslims. Will you be the strangers of the future?"

2

The Roots

Nowhere to Call Home

According to any good jihadi, Muslims today should be in a state of mourning. The source of bereavement is the destruction in recent history of the caliphate, the Islamic state requested by no less than God, and the failure of Muslims so far to rebuild it.

Notices of bereavement over the caliphate's demise and the delay in its resurrection can be found all across the virtual caliphate. They contribute to a sense that something is horribly wrong with the world and that only the most drastic acts can rectify it.

"There is no Khalifa [caliphate]. After 1300 years of Islamic rule. A glorious empire the world once feared," bemoans one such message. [1]

It goes on to lament the modern state in which the followers of Islam find themselves, the same followers who were "entrusted," in the words of the authors, with the final revelation of God.[2]

Islam, the religion "destined for the whole of humanity," is today in an unprecedented lull, the authors write, because the Muslim masses have been duped by their own regimes, described as "wooden-headed puppets."[3]

A grand conspiracy theory is laid out before the reader, the theory that a new form of dastardly colonialism has snaked its way into the Muslim world via Arab-Muslim regimes.

The resounding success of the conspirators, identified as the major powers of the West, is a completely humiliating development, the authors insist, all the more so because the majority of Muslims are not awake to the gravity of the situation.

"Their house is crumbling and their neighbors are laughing," the authors write, describing their view of the state of Muslims today.

These words appeared in an introduction to a book called *Defense of the Muslim Lands*, written by Sheikh Abdullah Azzam, the spiritual mentor to Osama Bin Laden. The text in the book first appeared as a *fatwa* (religious decree) that was issued by Azzam in 1979 as a response to the Soviet invasion of Afghanistan.

Azzam, a Palestinian cleric killed in Afghanistan in 1989, formed some of the ideas now central to the international jihadi campaign.

In *Defense of the Muslim Lands*, Azzam issued a set of orders, akin to an instruction manual, on how to reinstate the caliphate.

It has been translated into English, and in electronic book (e-book) form, it is easily and instantly transferable. It can now be read through the Adobe Acrobat Reader application from any computer. Azzam's introductory comments cited earlier were translated into English by "the Brothers in Ribatt," an unkown group of Islamists possibly based in Morocco, who uploaded Azzam's work. At a later stage, Islamists translated the text into English, making it available to English-speaking Muslims around the world.

The two paths central to the ideology of jihad have been presented to the young Muslim reading this book in the West: the path of disbelief, shared by conspiring enemies of Allah, and the path of jihad, for which Muslims must unite.

Azzam firmly stated the goals of jihad in the introduction: the establishment of a caliphate to rule the earth, and the annihilation of disbelief (and disbelievers) in Islam.

In his book, now spreading on the Internet at the speed of light, Azzam continued, explaining the purpose of the proposed Islamic state: to liberate the world. As with other extremist ideologues ready to maim and murder, jihadis believe they are doing humanity a favor.

In fact, jihadi ideologues believe they have been ordered to save humanity from its own ignorance and degeneracy. "Allah has chosen this religion to be a mercy for the worlds," Azzam wrote.[4]

At first, Muhammad attempted to reason with the unbelievers around him, expounding the new religion with "evidences and arguments."[5] But afterward, those who stubbornly refused to become Muslims became legitimate targets of violence.

Here jihad serves its purposes of salvaging humanity and picking up where the force of argument fails. Azzam's writings show how violence became entrenched as a sacred value at the center of the jihadi cult. While jihadis would have the world believe that their orders to fight go back to the seventh century, many of their ideas about modern jihad were formulated in the twentieth century.

Azzam used a range of Islamic *hadiths* (oral traditions attributed to Muhammad) to justify violence and to turn it into a central religious duty: "He [Allah] has provided sustenance from beneath the shadow of spears and has decreed humiliation and belittlement for those who oppose my order."[6]

Violence toward any individual, group, or state that opposes Islam is the modus operandi. The same approach is taken with other Muslims who disagree with this worldview. Azzam opined that Muslims opposed to jihad are no better than the infidels themselves. Perhaps they are even worse than infidels because, as jihadis believe, moderate Muslims have been exposed to Islam and yet still choose to stray from it.

Azzam, together with a host of ideologues, helped characterize the modern form of the Salafi movement. Salafism is the driving force behind all extreme Sunni movements. Although the term "Salafism" is vague and difficult to define, Islamists who identify themselves as Salafis hold themselves to be the only accurate interpreters of the Koran and believe in returning Islam to its "pure" state. They wish to turn the clock back to the time of Muhammad and the caliphate, the era they say saw the purest and most godly conduct of human beings.

The term "Salafi" means to precede or to go back, and it is linked to the Arabic name of the companions of Muhammad, called *al Salaf al salih*.[7] The Salafis, who comprised the first three generations of Muslims, learned Islam directly from Muhammad, meaning that they had the truest understanding of their religion, modern-day Salafis hold.[8]

Since that time, Islam has been corrupted by erroneous and nefarious interpretations that have led Muslims astray, and Salafis have developed a technique, which they call *Manhaj*, to filter out "true" Islam from false ideas. Manhaj is based on a fundamentalist and literal reading of the Koran and understanding of the *Sunna*, the normative way of life practiced and preached by Muhammad.[9]

Many of the jihadi chat rooms open today include the word "Sunna" in their room names, and the term is used like a password to confirm that Salafis are operating them.

Salafism's view that Muslims have been corrupted by impure schools of Islamic thought has evolved into the idea that Muslims have been corrupted by their own regimes. The charge is the same, but the target has now become governments and state systems. Thus, Salafis shifted from religious dogma to a radical, political ideology.

Today, the Salafi jihadis, the products of modern Salafi thought, face immense competition in the battleground of ideas. Democracy, market capitalism, and Western liberalism have infected Muslim minds, they say.

This is why driving out Western cultural ideas from Muslim minds is as important a goal for jihadis as forcing out Western military troops from Muslim lands.

The second stage—creating an Islamic state—is the end vision. It is a mission that some jihadis have prematurely declared to have accomplished.

In November 2006, Iraqi al Qaeda leader Sheikh Abu Hamza al-Muhajir said in an Internet message, "Today we announce the end of a stage of jihad and the start of a new one, in which we lay the first cornerstone of the Islamic caliphate project and revive the glory of religion."[10]

Al-Muhajir used the Internet to proclaim the establishment of the Islamic State of Iraq, which is "the state of Islam that will rule the law of Allah on people and lands, that will protect the core (center) of Islam and act as a solid shield for the Sunni people on the land of Iraq."[11]

In reality, the Islamic State of Iraq turned out to be a name for al Qaeda forces in Iraq who busied themselves attacking U.S. and Iraqi governments and Shiite targets.

The online declaration of an Islamic state is significant, however. Although jihadis are far from being at the stage where they can assert independence in any meaningful sense, the message does contain clues to a two-stage scheme. First, drive the West away from the House of Islam, and second, establish a transnational, ever-expanding Islamic state.

This two-staged plan can be found in the writings of Azzam. In *Defense of the Muslim Lands*, he spelled out two jihad scenarios, one for each phase in the plan.

According to Azzam, the first is an "offensive jihad," where the enemy "is attacked in his own territory." The crashing of two jetliners into New York's World Trade Center and the bombings of the London Underground trains are examples of offensive jihad.

In this type of war, "the Kuffar [infidels] are not gathering to fight the Muslims," Azzam emphasized. The duty to carry out unprovoked raids on infidels is *Fard Kifaya*, an obligation that, if taken on by a certain number of volunteers, absolves the rest of the Muslims from taking part. If, however, there are not enough volunteers, then all are in sin. When Muslims embark on offensive jihad, they must send "an army at least once a year to terrorise the enemies of Allah."[12]

Offensive jihad is vital for keeping infidels' countries at bay and under siege in order for the caliphate to be established. "It is a duty of the Imam [Islamic leader] to assemble and send out an army unit into the land of war once or twice every year. Moreover, it is the responsibility of the Muslim population to assist him, and if he does not send an army he is in sin," Azzam ruled.[13]

His writings make reference to the land of war, or Dar al-Harb, and it encompasses every inch of territory that is not part of the caliphate state of Islam—including, according to today's jihadi leaders, Arab-Muslim states that are accused of being too secular and corrupt.

No states today escape falling under the category of land of war. Until the caliphate is reestablished, the whole world is a land of war.

When jihadi soldiers bombed three hotels in Jordan in November 2005 and killed sixty people, they were obeying a command by the late Iraqi al Qaeda commander, Abu Musab al-Zarqawi, and operating under the assumption that the Kingdom of Jordan, an Arab country, was part of the land of war.

The second scenario is "defensive jihad." Azzam wrote that its aim is of "expelling the Kuffar [infidel] from our land," and it is *Fard Ayn,* a compulsory duty shared by everyone.[14]

If non-Muslims invade a Muslim land, defensive jihad automatically becomes a duty. Similarly, if an Imam declares defensive jihad, then Muslims must report for duty and enlist for the cause.

In defensive jihad, "the children will march forth without the permission of the parents, the wife without the permission of her husband, and the debtor without the permission of the creditor."[15]

If this first effort fails because the people "slacken, are indolent, or simply do not act," then the duty for defensive jihad "spreads in the shape of a circle from the nearest to the next nearest." A failure by a second wave of defensive jihadi fighters would result in the obligation falling "upon the people behind them, and on the people behind them, to march forward. This process continues until it becomes Fard Ayn [compulsory] upon the whole world."[16]

Iraq has become a focal point for defensive jihad, and the pattern of mobilization appears to follow Azzam's fatwa. Fighters from neighboring Syria, Jordan, and Saudi Arabia have poured into the country.

In the 1980s, Afghanistan was the center of gravity for jihadi fighters who were sure they were arriving to help found the next caliphate. Azzam, who was Palestinian in origin, directed his call for jihad away from Israel and the Palestinian territories. Instead, he instructed that "Muslims . . . should start their jihad in Afghanistan."[17]

Azzam surely knew his call would raise a few eyebrows—the Palestinian cause has long been a standard battle cry for Islamists—and he immediately provided an explanation for his stance.

It was not that "Afghanistan is more important than Palestine, not at all, Palestine is the foremost Islamic problem. It is the heart of the Islamic world, and it is a blessed land but, there are some reasons which make Afghanistan the starting point," he argued.[18]

Azzam was very excited by what was happening in Afghanistan. He feverishly reported how battles there between jihadis and Soviet forces had reached a level of intensity not seen in "recent Islamic history. . . . The Islamic flag being raised in Afghanistan is clear: and the aim is clear, 'to make Allah's words uppermost.' . . . 'The goal of this unification is to bring forth an Islamic state in Afghanistan.'"[19]

The jihad in Afghanistan was the top priority because it stood the best chance of founding a caliphate, Azzam concluded. Ultimately, Azzam's prediction proved to be correct, although he would not live to see it play out. A short-lived Islamic state, the Taliban, had reared its head.

But the Taliban state was fated for destruction. Its suicidal decision to host al Qaeda meant that it would become the first target of America's response to the offensive jihad attacks of September 11, 2001. Once again, jihadis had nowhere in the world to call home. The sounds of mourning again echoed among the holy warriors.

In his book *Milestones*, seminal Egyptian jihadi theorist, Sayyid Qutb, drove home the concept that the entire world was a land of war. First published in 1964, *Milestones* is considered the bible of the global jihadi movement. Since Azzam, Bin Laden, al-Zawahiri, and many other terrorist leaders have taken their cue from Qutb's ideas, and it would not be unreasonable to describe Qutb as the primary source for the jihadi worldview today.

His message is simple. A House of Islam is a country where only the most stringent and fundamentalist interpretation of Islam reigns as the law of the land and constitution.

"The rest of the world is the home of hostility [Dar al-Harb]. A Muslim can have only two possible relations with Dar al-Harb: peace with a contractual agreement, or war."[20]

A Muslim Has No Country

Much like Azzam's works, Qutb's book has been translated into English, uploaded onto an Adobe Acrobat file, and flashed from computer to computer around the world, eagerly read by new recruits to the jihad. *Milestones* may be banned in Egypt, but that is largely irrelevant to Internet users who can download it in seconds.

Qutb's bottom line can be summed up in his statement: "A Muslim has no country except that part of the earth where the Shari'ah [Islamic law] of God is established."[21]

Qutb conjured a utopian vision of how a caliphate should look. It is a state in which "human relationships are based on the foundation of relationship with God."[22] Until that state is established, he added, Muslims must consider themselves homeless.

Nationality, family, friendship—all factors that make up identities—must be cast away in favor of a bond established with other believers "through their relationship with God."[23]

Qutb dismissed the most fundamental relationships a person can have with one's parents, siblings, or spouse by stating that these are worthless if they are not based on faith.

The same message would appear decades later in jihadi recruitment videos.

Egypt, Jordan, Saudi Arabia, and Pakistan are in an unending battle to safeguard their national security from Qutb's followers. And their legitimacy is under constant assault. Qutb ruled that these are not bona fide Islamic states, describing them instead as pretender states. Jihadis claim that they do not have the Koran as their constitutions and that they do not care about Islam. The only solution is to replace these states with a real Islamic caliphate.

In true Salafi fashion, Qutb invoked Muhammad in order to show that his position is divinely sanctioned. Although Muhammad was born in Mecca and had relatives and homes in the city, that did not prevent him from going to war with Mecca, Qutb recounted.

Once again, the key message is repeated: the society around the "awoken" jihadi recruit is corrupt, and one should break all loyalties to it.

"[T]he soil of Mecca did not become Dar-al-Islam [House of Islam] for him and his followers until it surrendered to Islam and the Shari'ah became operative in it. This, and only this is Islam."[24] One's soil, race, lineage, tribe, and family have nothing to do with Islam, Qutb believed.

Qutb gave his readers the litmus test with which to identify an infidel country masquerading as a Muslim state. This is defined as "any country which fights the Muslim because of his belief and prevents him from practicing his religion, and in which the Shari'ah is suspended."[25] Such a country qualifies for the status of Dar al-Harb, even if a jihadi's family or national ethnic group resides in it, or if a jihadi has financially invested in the country (before he became indoctrinated).

Conversely, a state in which Islam is "dominant" is a House of Islam, even if the jihadi has no blood relatives there or links to its population. With a wave of his radical literary wand, Qutb laid waste to the legitimacy of Muslims living in non-Muslim countries as minorities. He said that Islam cannot exist as a minority religion in any land, nor can it exist alongside any other system. Islam can only be the state ruling system. In fact, an Islam that exists as a minority rather than a dominant religion might as well not exist at all.

Another weapon in the arsenal of religious terms used by jihadis is the term *jahiliya*, meaning the age of darkness before Islam enlightened the world. Qutb argued that Islam can never coexist with ideas emanating from the impure age of pre-Islamic ignorance, the time before humanity had its "eyes opened" by Islam.

Islamic history is divided into two distinct eras: the pre-enlightenment age of jahiliya, before the world heard Muhammad's message, and the post-enlightenment time, which began from Muhammad's preaching of Islam in the seventh century until today. Ingeniously, jihadi ideologues use the term "jahiliya" today to tar all ideas that they view as non-Islamic and impure. Democracy, globalization, and secularism are all modern forms of jahiliya, Qutb argued, training a politicized Salafi lens onto the cornerstones of Western civilization. So-called Muslim states have been infected with these jahiliya ideas, Qutb claimed.

"It is not the function of Islam to compromise with the concepts of jahiliya which are current in the world or to coexist in the same land together with a *jahili* [age of darkness] system. This was not the case when it [Islam] first appeared in the world, nor will it be today or in the future. . . . Jahiliya, to whatever period it belongs, is jahiliya; that is, deviation from the worship of one God," Qutb ruled.[26]

According to Qutb, Egypt, Saudi Arabia, Jordan, Pakistan, and every other Muslim state are undoubtedly part of the enemy jahiliya system. They do not cut it as real Muslim states. Whether it is secular Egypt and Syria, or Saudi Arabia and its alliance with the "satanic" United States, they are all taken out of the house of Islam category and placed into the land of war. Needless to say, the Western world is the chief supplier of jahiliya.

When jahiliya rules a person's psyche, it lures its victim through "human desires," Qutb warned, blinding the person to God's justice. But the good news is that Islam has the answer. It provides a system of divine laws that does not suffer from human interference and that is totally free from human biases. In his writings, Qutb spoke of the psychological boost that absolute religious belief bestows to fanatics. He described how internalizing the jihadi worldview grants the new recruit "confidence and power . . . the confidence of a man who knows that he is with the truth, while what the people have is falsehood."[27] Bluntness, unapologetic aggression, and a scornful view of compromise must characterize communication with the unbelievers, Qutb insisted. "We will be extremely outspoken with them," he wrote.[28]

Qutb affirmed that Muhammad, the first Muslim, took this tone with the non-Muslims around him, and it is therefore the right tone to take today. Muslims who do not yet know they are in a state of jahiliya need to be told they are living in ignorance and that God wants to purify them. They need to be told that their customs are defiling. And they need to be shown that "Islam will change your concepts, your modes of living, and your values; will raise you to another life so that you will look upon the life you are now living with disgust."[29] Moderate Muslims who "feel the need" to apologize and justify their faith are incapable of presenting Islam to people, Qutb argued. Muslims who do not support jihad are "hollow and full of contradictions," stuck deep in a state of jahiliya.[30]

These writings have become the foundation of every radical Sunni Islamist organization. Although Egyptian, Qutb authored sections in his works to which

Muslims living in the West can relate, such as his two-year stay in the United States from 1948 to 1950. Qutb told his readers about his experiences encountering jahiliya in the heartland of infidelity. He described his absolute disgust with America's "shaky religious beliefs, its social and economic modes, and its immoralities."[31]

Qutb pointed a contemptuous finger at Catholicism, capitalism, and America's "materialistic attitude which deadens the spirit." He openly mocked Christianity, which is "agreeable neither to reason nor to conscience," and lashed out at "this capitalism with its monopolies, its usury and whatever else is unjust in it." It is an extended rant with an unmistakably violent undertone. He also described the women's emancipation movement as a "vulgarity" because it places women in positions that are "contrary to the demands of practical life."[32]

After spewing out paragraph upon paragraph of venomous censure, Qutb directed his readers back to Islam, "with its logic, beauty, humanity and happiness, which reaches the horizons to which man strives but does not reach." Americans blushed when they looked at Western life in the light of Islam, Qutb claimed. After his visit to the United States, Qutb found it even more difficult to understand moderate Muslims "who are defeated before this filth in which jahiliya is steeped, even to the extent that they search for resemblances to Islam among this rubbish heap of the West, and also among the evil and dirty materialism of the East."[33]

The chasm between Islam and all things not Islamic is too great for any bridge, and Muslims, along with the rest of humanity, must choose, irrespective of "whether they reside in a so-called Islamic country and consider themselves Muslims or they are outside of the 'Islamic' country."[34]

This declaration of war on the entire world no longer appears as print on paper; it is no longer bound in a book that is banned from several states. It is now being e-mailed, downloaded, and forwarded. It is reverberating across the virtual caliphate and is used to call up more and more Muslims to fight the jihad.

Qutb's Army

After learning of Qutb's ideas, Egyptian Islamists declared their country to be in a deep state of jahiliya and repeatedly attempted to overthrow the Egyptian government. They succeeded in assassinating the Egyptian president, Anwar Sadat, in 1981, whose unforgivable sin was signing a peace treaty with Israel. The Egyptian al-Jihad organization failed, however, in its mission to ascend to power in Egypt, despite numerous attempts to topple the secular regime led by Hosni Mubarak, Sadat's successor.

Meanwhile, Saudi Arabia faced its own Islamist problem in the form of the increasingly radicalized Osama Bin Laden.

Bin Laden, who studied under Azzam—himself deeply inspired by Qutb—viewed his organization *al Qaeda*, or "The Base," as the rightful heir to power in Saudi Arabia, rather than the corrupt Saudi government, which allowed U.S. soldiers to set foot on the Arabian peninsula, considered holy ground by Islam and off limits to infidels who defile it with their presence. In Saudi Arabia, Bin Laden hoped to establish a caliphate. As with the Egyptian al-Jihad, he failed as well.

In Afghanistan, during the war against invading Soviets and the subsequent Taliban rule, jihadis from Saudi Arabia and Egypt met and gelled into a single international organization: al Qaeda. The organization's top tier represents this Egyptian-Saudi fusion: Bin Laden is a Saudi, and his deputy, Ayman al-Zawahiri, is an Egyptian.

Indeed, Afghanistan can be described as an Islamist melting pot, from which a lethal stew emerged.

In 1996 Bin Laded declared a fatwa. As with Qutb's followers, he declared his own country, Saudi Arabia, or "the land of the two Holy Sites," to be a U.S. puppet following American orders and persecuting Islamic scholars. "We, myself and my group, have suffered some of this injustice ourselves; we have been prevented from addressing the Muslims. We have been pursued in Pakistan, Sudan and Afghanistan, hence this long absence on my part."[35]

Like Azzam, Bin Laden was very excited by what was taking place in Afghanistan, where the Taliban state had already been established. "But by the Grace of Allah, a safe base is now available in the high Hindukush mountains in Khurasan." This is where the mighty infidel Soviet superpower had been defeated, Bin Laden exclaimed. In an ominous warning to the United States, he added, "And the myth of the superpower was withered in front of the *Mujahideen* [holy warriors'] cries of *Allahu Akbar* [God is greater]."[36]

Jihadis fought a hard war to clear Afghanistan of the Soviets, and they reveled in their new found home, a place in which they could establish a caliphate after decades of failure and seek to expand it. "Today we work from the same mountains to lift the iniquity that had been imposed on the *Ummah* [Islamic nation] by the Zionist-

Crusader alliance," Bin Laden declared. Five years later, his physical "safe base" was destroyed. The next base Bin Laden's followers founded would be immune to fighter jets and ground troops.

Islamists Splintered

The writings of Qutb and Azzam form the ideological basis of al Qaeda. They lay out a roadmap for future jihadis and instruct them to wage an armed struggle to do away with counterfeit Muslim regimes and work towards the installation of the caliphate. But not all Islamists who wish to found the caliphate propose the immediate taking up of arms, and not all of them are the ideological descendants of Qutb. Other movements have also reached the conclusion that the time for building the caliphate is nigh and have developed their views independently of Egyptian jihadi thinkers and Saudi Islamist revolutionaries.

While there is no consensus among analysts on whether Hizb ut-Tahrir (the Party of God) is an inherently violent organization, it is undoubtedly one of the most formative procaliphate movements around. Like al Qaeda, Hizb ut-Tahrir would go on to forge a base for itself on the Internet. Hizb ut-Tahrir was founded by Taqi Nabhani, a Jordanian-Palestinian Islamic jurist. In 1952 Nabhani asked the Jordanian Interior Ministry for permission to establish "a political party with Islam as its ideology."[37] Instantly realizing that the proposed party was taking aim at its own sovereignty, the Jordanian monarchical regime turned down the proposal and banned Hizb ut-Tahrir.[38] It would be the beginning of many prohibitions. After being banned from virtually every Arab state, Hizb operatives fled for safer shores. Many washed up on the shores of Britain. One of the most fascinating accounts of membership in the organization came from Ed Husain, author of *The Islamist*, an inside look at Islamist life in the United Kingdom.

Husain describes a feverish organizational work ethic within Hizb in the early 1990s, driven by the absolute and messianic belief that the caliphate will surely soon arrive. The same attitudes would soon be on display on dozens of websites owned and operated by Hizb ut-Tahrir. Although Bin Laden and his deputy al-Zawahiri owed some of their ideas to Hizb, al Qaeda and Hizb ut-Tahrir are clearly separate Islamist organizations, both vying for the caliphate in different ways. Unlike al Qaeda, Hizb ut-Tahrir does not place jihad as its main vehicle for achieving the caliphate. Instead, Hizb believes in da'wa, aggressive proselytizing and preaching, as the means to build the caliphate.

But, as Husain notes, the two organizations are not as far apart as they seem. As one Hizb ut-Tahrir member told him, "Qutb referred to being in discussions with a certain group of Muslims in the first letters he wrote to his family. Those letters, later published as *Milestones*, were the ideas of Hizb ut-Tahrir."[39]

Indeed, Qutb was deeply influenced by Nabhani's ideas, which were contained in Nabhani's book, *The Way for Revival.* In it, Nabhani stressed the identity of the Muslim *ummah*, or "nation." The Islamic nation has been fractured into artificial nationalities, such as Turks, Jordanians and Malaysians, and only the caliphate had the power to reunite the Muslims, housing the integrated ummah under one roof. The call for a complete destruction of the nation-state system, today being used online to lure recruits into joining the jihad, was first made by Nabhani in the 1950s. "The Hizb is organic," an operative of the group told Husain in a prophetic comment.[40] "Our ideas do not require offices, mosques, schools, charities, institutions for dissemination. They spread like wildfire."[41] They spread faster than wildfire online.

Any discussion of the Islamist forces at play on the net today would be incomplete without a look at Wahhabism. In the eighteenth century, a Muslim preacher by the name of Ibn Abd al-Wahhab began preaching a new idea to the Bedouins of Najd, in modern-day Saudi Arabia.[42]

Al-Wahhab blamed the decline of the Muslims on poisonous European ideas such as secularism and liberalism, as well as traditional Islam, and prescribed a puritanical, fundamentalist faith system as the cure. Al-Wahhab and his followers constantly emphasized monotheism, and looked down on traditional Islamic practice. He also emphasized jihad in a way that was rare during that time.[43] Both Wahhabism and Salafism have condemned traditional Islam and adopted a radical reading of Islam, although according to terrorism analyst Trevor Stanley, Salafism differs from Wahhabism over the question of reconciling Islam with modernity: Salafis try to realize this idea, whereas Wahhabis do not.[44] While most would associate Wahhabism with Saudi Arabia, which is indeed the heartland of this school of Islamic thought, Stanley believes the Saudi kingdom, under King Faysal, has in effect adopted a mix of Wahhabism and Salafism, creating a hybrid radical stream. For jihadis determined to overthrow the Kingdom's government, Saudi Arabia's state ideology remains unforgivably moderate and willing to collaborate with the infidel superpower, the United States.

3
Going Online

The period shortly following the September 11 attacks—during which the destruction of the Taliban and al Qaeda's base took place—is the juncture of history in which the virtual caliphate really began.

At this time global electronic communications exploded onto the world stage and became the dominant media they are today. From its rapid growth in the 1990s, the Internet was poised to become the most efficient and direct way to communicate at the speed of light.

The Internet's key characteristics are its accessibility and anonymity. Websites can be constructed in hours, and the audience is virtually limitless.

Jihadis had just lost their latest physical safe house in Afghanistan. Now, no country afforded them the freedom to openly recruit and train an army, conduct mass indoctrinations, and plot to bring down governments in order to establish the caliphate. Al Qaeda loyalists quickly began seeking digital refuge.

One reason why we can speak of a virtual caliphate is that jihadis use the Internet to discuss how their future state will look. The details of the planning are remarkable and include meticulously drawn diagrams of the would-be caliphate government, webpage after webpage of explanation on the various ministries' roles, and heated debates on where the caliphate should exist.

The Islamic Thinkers website was founded by American Islamists, who made available for download a magazine titled *Islamic Revival*, which is dedicated to the reestablishment of the caliphate.

The magazine's ninth volume describes how the infidels conspired to destroy the caliphate in 1924. That year, the Ottoman Empire, the last caliphate in history, drew its last breaths. The man behind the caliphate's collapse was secular Turkish leader, Mustafa Kemal (later known as *Atatürk*, or "Father of the Turks"). Although Kemal was a Muslim, *Islamic Revival*'s authors adamantly believe that Turkish Muslims did not really destroy the caliphate, but rather European Christians, who did so by employing an agent—Mustafa Kemal.

"The situation now is that the Islamic Caliphate in Turkey is dead and will never rise again, because we have destroyed its moral strength, the Caliphate and Islam."[1] *Islamic Revival* attributed this quote to Lord Curzon, the British foreign minister who was in office during the year of the caliphate's demise. Allegedly, he made these comments before the House of Commons in 1924.

"We must put an end to anything which brings about any Islamic unity between the sons of the Muslims. As we have already succeeded in finishing off the Caliphate, so we must ensure that there will never arise again unity for the Muslims, whether it be intellectual or cultural unity," another top-ranking British foreign minister is cited as saying.[2]

These quotes appear only on jihadi websites and are highly dubious. The quotes are reminiscent of the Protocols of the Elders of Zion—a forged anti-Semitic "protocol" released by Czarist Russia in the twentieth century, aimed at demonizing Jews by attributing to them plots of world domination. In this case, jihadis have produced "Protocols of the Elders of Britain", so-called proof that Islam's enemies planned the caliphate's demise. According to the websites, these same enemies are today hell-bent on defending their achievement and plot to keep the caliphate from ever rising again.

In addition to uncovering this so-called conspiracy, the *Islamic Revival* online magazine bemoans the fact that the caliphate's rebirth is not at the forefront of most Muslims' minds. Why, the website asks, do Muslims not "even know about their true ruling system? . . . They've never even heard the word 'caliphate' uttered in any discussion related to their revival?"[3]

The website argues that a plot has been set in motion by the British to brainwash the Muslims into forgetting about the caliphate and to convince the Muslims to adopt "their system."[4] Democracy and liberalism are thus presented as the tools of a neo-imperialist mind-control conspiracy against Muslim unity. Muslims who promote these values are little more than indoctrinated stooges, or worse, active conspirators, such as Mustafa Kemal, a "British agent and traitor."[5] Kemal is portrayed in *Islamic Revival* as a Christian agent who killed the state-system ordained by God.

On March 3 of every year, soldiers and commanders of the jihad bow their head in mourning, and the virtual flag of jihadism flies half-mast, for it was the day in 1924 when the caliphate was officially destroyed in Turkey "by the enemies of Allah [the infidels] and their slave Mustafa Kemal Ataturk, may Allah's wrath, curse, and punishments be upon him."[6]

It was also the day when the camp of Islam, the symbol of monotheism and "submission to the commands of our lord," opposed only by infidels, ceased to be. Muhammad prophesized this dire development, *Islamic Revival* says.[7]

Thanks to the deliberately planted mass ignorance of the caliphate among Muslims today, the *Islamic Revival* online magazine sets out to prove that the caliphate's blueprints can be found in the Koran, which has ordered that the caliphate be reinstated without delay. The website places in bold sections where the authors believe Allah speaks of the caliphate. A few examples: "Allah says: . . . Indeed, we have revealed to you the book with the truth so that you may **rule** between mankind by that which Allah has shown you (Standard English version of Koran, 4:105). So **rule between them** by that which Allah has revealed, and follow not their desires (4:49). Whosoever does not **rule by that which Allah has revealed**, they are disbelievers, oppressors and evil doers. (5:44–47)"[8] (emphasis in original).

According to *Islamic Revival*, the word "rule" as it appears above demonstrates that Allah intended his followers to construct a state and to turn the Koran into its constitution in order to run the daily life of its citizens. This understanding stems from the reading the word "rule" to mean a political state.

Next, in what is a truly unique use of the Internet, *Islamic Revival* uploaded a state plan in the form of an illustration to show how the proposed caliphate would look. A line model depicting a hierarchal structure appears on the screen. At the top of the model is "sovereignty," belonging exclusively to God.[9] Beneath is *al-Khaleefah* (head of the caliphate). He is appointed by the People's Council that represents the masses and places limits on the list of nominees vying to become *al-Khaleefah*.

Once in position, *al-Khaleefah* will appoint a chief judge, administrative assistants, governors, an *amir al-Jihad* (head of armed forces), deputies, and executive assistants. The model becomes a sprawling web, mapping out the structure of the regime.

The amir al-Jihad is given access to enormous power by these state planners. He has direct reign over the ministries of war, foreign affairs, interior, and industry. Deputies of the caliphate's ruler supervise the ministries of health, education, and agriculture. Clearly, in its quest to broaden its borders, the caliphate will be at war with the infidels for a long time to come, and the amir al-Jihad will need access to all of the caliphate's resources in order to coordinate the conquest. For this reason, he has overarching control of so many ministries.

This model of the caliphate is being sent from computer to computer on the World Wide Web. And one could argue that the state's various ministries are already beginning to come alive on the Internet, as they take on some functions which will be discussed in later chapters.

Islamic Revival has the feel of a Hizb ut-Tahrir–managed website, with its derision of Muslim disunity and contempt of the notion of separate Arab-Muslim nationalities and identities. Similar to Hizb, the website does not call for violent holy war, but instead uses the Internet for missionizing and "educating" users about the coming caliphate. *Islamic Revival* derived its name from the all-important book written by Hizb ut-Tahrir's founder, Taqi Nabhani, *The Way for Revival* (as discussed in chapter two).

The split among Islamists on whether to focus on da'wa or jihad is noticeable among the online disciples of the Muslim Brotherhood and al Qaeda. These two organizations are at odds over whether to launch the jihad now or later, and the split is very real, often causing bitter feuds online.

No longer accessible, an online forum called Muntadaa was used by British Muslims affiliated with al Qaeda to hold uninterrupted, heated discussions on building the caliphate.[10] In February 2006, a forum member posted a transcript of a sermon delivered by an Islamic preacher.

The talk was titled "fighting to establish an Islamic state," and the sermon was delivered by Jamaal ud-Deen Zarabozo. Zarabozo was trying to answer a question that was at the heart of the al Qaeda–Muslim Brotherhood split: Can Islamists take up arms and form an army before actually founding the caliphate? Can they create a stateless military? "If we are striving to create an Islamic State, do we have the right by *sharia* to fight on behalf of establishing an Islamic State?" he asked.[11] Zarabozo's answer would spark irate responses.

The preacher acknowledged that some respected jurists have ruled that fighting precaliphate battles is not allowed.[12] This anti-jihad school of thought bases its belief on the fact that Muhammad and his companions were not permitted by Islam to fight until they founded the first Islamic state. The first mission is to teach the people about Islam, Zarabozo said. "Al Albaani [a prominent twentieth-century Islamic scholar] says that if you put Islam in your hearts, the Islamic State and Islamic society will thereafter be formed."[13]

The belief that Islam needs to be firmly implanted in society ("in your hearts") before the caliphate's creation can be viable is a concise sum-up of the Muslim Brotherhood ideology. It also flies in the face of al Qaeda's ideas.

Founded by Hassan al-Banna in the smoky coffeehouses of Cairo in 1928, the Muslim Brotherhood believed that instant jihad was useless so long as the masses were not properly following Islam. There would be no point in establishing an Islamic state, they reasoned, if a self-aware and educated Islamic nation did not first exist to populate it. The Muslim Brothers therefore dedicated themselves to the mission of "implanting Islam in the hearts" of Muslims in order to make them more pious. Once an Islamic society was formed in Egypt, as well as other Muslim states, an Islamic revolution would naturally erupt, and a caliphate would easily be born. Better yet, a caliphate government can be elected into office without the need to fire a single bullet, Muslim Brothers say today. Outside of Muslim-majority states, the Brothers have set up branches designed to propagate their ideology and bring non-Muslims to Islam. The branches operate across Europe, in countries such as Britain, France, Italy and Germany, as well as the United States. Keen to avoid identifying themselves as part of the Muslim Brotherhood, the activists who run the branches have created a plethora of cover names for their organizations. The branches are closely monitored by the Global Muslim Brotherhood Daily Report website.[14]

The main difference between the Muslim Brotherhood and the Egyptian al-Jihad organization, which sprang up in the 1980s and evolved into the modern al Qaeda, is that al-Jihad focuses on instant holy war. Al-Jihad members believe that the caliphate must first be created through violent revolution and that Islamizing society is the second goal. Muslim Brotherhood members disagree, arguing that that position is too radical and out of touch with reality. Bids for armed revolution have failed too many times in Egypt to be seriously considered as an option, the Brotherhood members say in response. And it has failed because not enough of the masses believe in the caliphate, leaving the revolutionaries without a popular base of support.

This fracture in ideologies between the Muslim Brotherhood and al Qaeda spread out to other Muslim organizations around the world over the past three decades

Today, Islamists are still split between the Muslim Brotherhood approach of making Muslims more religious and al Qaeda's call to wage jihad now.

In Britain, the Muslim Association of Britain (MAB) follows the Muslim Brotherhood path, while al Qaeda's "representation" in the United Kingdom, formally known as Al-Muhajiroun, and its various subgroupings that are constantly renaming themselves (such as al-Ghurabaa, the Saved Sect, and the Followers of ahl Us-Sunnah wal-Jamaa'ah) follow the al Qaeda model. On the Internet, the British Muslim Brothers and al Qaeda followers spend much of their time delegitimizing one another.

Returning to Zarabozo's online sermon, he concluded that the Muslim Brothers are simply too naïve to believe that da'wa alone will set the caliphate in motion. "From the verses of Koran and *hadeeth*, we know that the infidels hate Islam, and won't be happy until we give up Islam," he said. Missionizing is insufficient to overcome the level of nefarious and organized intent that keeps Muslims down, Zarabozo opined. It would be impractical to assume that "the infidels will just watch us quietly and let it [the founding of the caliphate] happen."[15]

Zarabozo came down on the side of al Qaeda in this debate. But the way he reached his position left much to be desired, according to one member of the web forum, a jihadi leader known as Abu Baraa.

Posting a message in the forum underneath the sermon, Abu Baraa wrote that he found the sermon lacking in jihadi zeal: "The article is good in general but i [*sic*] do not agree with the terminology here, it is a mistake to even mention practicality."[16]

There is no such thing as impracticality when one is carrying out God's orders, Abu Baraa affirmed, and God alone can decide how the caliphate will be founded. It matters not whether the infidels "watch quietly or loudly," for "the Islamic state will be established however Allah wishes and neither the jihad nor the *da'wa* can stop until it is."[17]

It later became known that Abu Baraa was an alias used by Omar Brooks, a Jamaican-British electrician who converted to Islam in the United Kingdom and became a local jihadi leader. Brooks would later be arrested for one of several confrontations with British police.

Abu Baraa objected to the online sermon even though it called for jihad to establish the caliphate, because the sermon portrayed the jihad as the better of two evils. For Abu Baraa, and the majority of al Qaeda supporters and members around the world, instant jihad and the construction of the caliphate are ideological goals in their own right, not a choice between what is practical or not. His view is a typical one among jihadi ideologues preaching on the Internet. Jihad is the goal.

Jihad Net

The content of the aforementioned online conversation could easily lead to a prison sentence and even torture in an Arab-Asian-Muslim country for those involved, especially if its security forces conclude that the participants were plotting to establish the caliphate in place of the country itself—as is usually the case. Because they take place on the Internet, however, these discussions are usually out of security forces' grasp.

More and more jihadis have realized that the Internet is the ideal location for them to disseminate their blueprints for the caliphate. An increasing number of jihad attacks originated from indoctrination, conversations, and detailed attack plans on the Internet.

Aaron Weisburd, author of the Internet Haganah website, systematically tracks down and works toward the closure of jihadi websites. Weisburd, later mentioned in chapter 10, has been the subject of numerous jihadi threats, and at times the source of objections from the authorities for his unrelenting campaign. Weisburd has had years of experience with jihadi websites.

In an interview for this book conducted through e-mailed questions and answers, this author asked Weisburd whether terrorist attacks were clearly linked to the online jihadi presence. "There is no wall, no dividing line, nothing separating online jihadist activity from off-line/real-world jihadist activity (i.e. terrorism). The two are inseparable," he said in an email.[18]

Weisburd recounted how one prominent participant of an online jihadi forum was arrested in London after police suspected him of being a member of an international Islamic terrorist ring that was plotting bombings. Such cases are becoming increasingly common.

In fact, the jihadi Internet network has grown at such a fast pace that in January 2007 al Qaeda announced the release of its very own software. It allows members and new recruits to communicate using an al Qaeda–made encryption program meant to keep the virtual caliphate's communications out of range of governments and their prying security agencies.

On January 1, 2007, a new milestone was reached when one of al Qaeda's Internet spokesperson departments, the Global Islamic Media Front (GIMF), released an encryption program called Mujahideen Secrets.[19]

GIMF is responsible for disseminating al Qaeda's communications and propaganda online. Within the realm of the virtual caliphate, GIMF is at the heart of its ministry of information.

Al Qaeda heralded its new encryption program as "'the first Islamic computer program for secure exchange (of information) on the Internet,'" providing users with "the five best encryption algorithms, and with symmetrical encryption keys (256 bit), asymmetrical encryption keys (2048 bit) and data compression (tools)."[20]

The Mujahideen Secrets program may well represent the next stage in the virtual caliphate's evolution, allowing issues such as attack plans, weapons assembly, and recruitment to take place in an even more unrestricted virtual environment. Jihadi preachers were not slow in spreading the word to followers about Mujahideen Secrets, urging them to obtain the program and use it in order to continue the war.

Al Qaeda members have been ordering Muslims onto the Internet since 2003 when a seminal Internet message was released by Ahmad Al Hatheq Bin Allah, a previously unknown jihadi source. Bin Allah called on followers to take to Western Internet forums in order to "portray the truth convincingly through visual or oral arguments, especially as it concerns Iraq, Afghanistan, Palestine, and Chechnya."[21]

Bin Allah's call is an attempt at online da'wa. The mission: to convert the Internet's non-Muslims areas, the online Dar al-Harb, to jihadism.

Bin Allah's statement also contains a threat against the American people. He warned that if Americans do not turn against their government, "the American people themselves will be to blame for attacks brought upon them."[22] The threat is not an empty one; tens of thousands of people have been recruited and provided training—all online—to form sleeper cells for attacks. The websites responsible for this phenomenon make up the virtual caliphate's most important ministry.

4
The Ministry of War

"In Jihad there is always an Amir [commander] al Jihad, especially for offensive jihad. In defensive jihad, there is a permit at the start of fighting to fight however you can, but eventually you must organize and appoint an Amir. The Amir has titles, like Al Ghazi (the raider), Al Mansur."

—*UK jihadi website, 2005*

The virtual caliphate's ministry of war is dedicated to the indoctrination, recruitment, and training of Muslim soldiers for holy war. Without this type of web activity, there would be no virtual caliphate, and the number of jihadis and terrorist attacks around the world—"the offline jihad" as jihadi website hunter Aaron Weisburd calls it—would be far lower than the current levels seen today.

While all elements of the virtual caliphate reverberate with jihad propaganda, it is the ministry of war that actively seeks out young Muslims and preys on their minds. Its aim is to turn them into members of terrorist cells and make them eager to commit mass murder and suicide. Once the indoctrination and training are complete, these members will either travel abroad to fight or form cells ready for activation. In some cases, a command to activate these sleeper cells is delivered online. Before that time, the members will likely spend their time in a jihadi virtual setting where they recruit other members or replenish their levels of hatred for infidels and desire to sacrifice their lives for the caliphate's establishment.

The Paltalk chat room described at the beginning of chapter 1 is an excellent example of a major recruitment drive by the virtual caliphate's ministry of war, UK branch. It represents a "point of entry" website, aimed at Muslims who may feel sympathy for al Qaeda's message but are not fully indoctrinated. As they spend increasing amounts of time in the jihadi setting, participants in a point of entry website become fully open to the jihadi message.

Members of jihadi online environments such as the Paltalk chat room will learn to despise Western culture and are taught that the rulers of Saudi Arabia, for example, are infidels. They will be directed to download documents from jihadi English-language sites that indoctrinate them with lessons of historic Islamic conquests.

Potential recruits are told by jihadi websites that the mission of true Muslims is to "carry the Message of Islam to the whole of mankind. Therefore, the Muslims had to be in touch with the world."[1]

In essence, this is the task of the caliphate. "It was inevitable that the state would conquer other countries and achieve this with great success," young jihadis are told. "These conquests were merely the implementation of an Islamic obligation."[2]

Global conquest is merely a divine command to spread God's truth to the world, according to the message. Hence, Muslims should look back on the Islamic conquests and exponential growth of the Muslim empire in the years following the death of Muhammad with great pride and seek to resurrect such an empire today. The reason the caliphate succeeded then was because of "the seed of its establishment," which "was destined to bear a universal state, not a local one, because its doctrine is a universal one."[3]

As young Muslims come back time after time to these websites, they will hear one consistent message, as repeated by Abu Baraa on February 13, 2006, in the Paltalk chat room: "The jihad has become Fard Ayn [compulsory] upon all Muslims, everywhere. Every single Muslim according to their capability."[4]

Abu Baraa told his listeners that the jihad can be carried out either physically or verbally. He explained that verbal jihad—the da'wa—could also be used "to establish the caliphate. All of this is part of your duties."[5]

Hating Democracy

As part of the indoctrination program, participants are taught to develop a burning hatred for the West, non-Muslims, Muslims who disagree with al Qaeda, homosexuals, Jews, Christians, Hindus, Buddhists, the United States, Israel, Britain, Europe, and many other people and places. Anyone who is not a jihadi is a hated enemy, though some targets make for higher profile attractions of hatred than others.

Online, jihadis present such hatred as being divinely sanctioned, a necessary step to victory. A large percentage of the virtual caliphate's indoctrination program is aimed at sniping at the West. The Western concept of individual liberties is one of the most commonly attacked ideas within the virtual caliphate.

An article on the IslamBase website, called "The Plague of the West," claims that the media portrays Western freedom as "the ultimate solution for the salvation of mankind and the places to find 'paradise' on earth since they permit the freedom of man to do as they wish."[6]

But the reality of Western daily life shows how false and rotten such ideas really are, the recruits are told. "If these Western countries were really as good as they are portrayed then one would surely not expect there to be any hardship, crime nor criminality since the individuals who were living in society would have no need for such untoward activities," IslamBase argues.[7]

Instead of utopia, a bleak existence characterizes so-called free nations. "When one switches on the television in the West, one almost receives a constant barrage of news regarding crimes and criminal activities."[8] The fact that the Western world is not a utopia proves it is a condemned, defective, and inferior model, jihadis say, unlike the caliphate.

Secularism and democracy do not escape the website's wrath either. Choosing new leaders every four years is dangerous, because depraved and sinister anti-Islamic governments can be voted into power. Democracy is a slippery slope, which starts with legalizing alcohol and gambling, and then goes on to approve the killing of Muslims, wars in Afghanistan and Iraq, homosexuality, and same-sex marriages.

The West is not only immoral, according to jihadi propaganda, it is also plotting a war against Islam, which is why Islam needs jihadis, the vanguard of its defenders.

The demonization of the West is constant and relentless. The West is morally sick and needs to be destroyed, online messages cry out. Its immorality is so extreme that Western law books have had to include prohibitions of male-on-male rape and rape by minors. Such laws go to show "the sick mindset of the West and their liberating ideology of freedom."[9] The West is synonymous with decadent evil.

Sodomy, bestiality, and incest are crimes that are acceptable in non-Islamic societies, jihadi websites communicate. Dating agencies, escort agencies, and prostitution are widespread, they warn. Women are degraded into sex objects and are used "to sell almost anything. Billboards will openly display nudity, and magazines, newspapers, films, soaps and dramas are full of it," an online message called "Homosexuality Today, Paedophile Tomorrow" stated.[10]

It is up to jihadis to put a stop to the perilous Westernization of Muslims. In the name of advancement, freedom, and individual rights, Western ideas are infiltrating Muslim minds. "Is this the type of society which truly offers prosperity, development and security for its inhabitants?" asks IslamBase.[11] The time has come for Muslims to take action to avoid having to live in societies infected by the Western plague.

Moral degradation is bad enough, but conspiring to destroy Islam is clearly the West's most dangerous intention, which is why an army needs to be formed, jihadi websites continue.

"Democracy=terrorism," was the title of one message posted on the now-defunct Saved Sect website. The message said that the West used terrorism to recreate democracies in Muslim lands, with Iraq being the clearest example.[12] Iraqis did not choose their political reality, nor did Afghanis. Instead, the United States stormed these Muslim lands, using its military might to spread democracy to these countries—against the will of their inhabitants.

This rhetoric, directed at Muslims living in the West, shows them that the democracy of Western nations in which they live is phony and part of a plan to destroy Islam. For jihadis, democratization is another word for crusaders who have replaced the symbol of the cross with the symbol of democracy. Democratic countries wish to dominate the world by making "their system of governance dominant over the world by forcing others to live their lives according to it," the Saved Sect warned.[13]

Another Islamist website, Milla Ibraheem, released a statement titled: "Western Society: A Culture of paganism And disbelief." Milla Ibraheem frets over its belief that so many Muslims "have failed to recognize the evil of Western society, and have failed to recognize how it has plundered into the depths of kufr [infidelity] and shirk [polytheism]." The rhetoric even targets a seemingly innocuous thing, romantic love, as an example of Western evil. Romantic love is a form of paganism, the website explains, because it encourages the love of someone other than Allah. Young Muslims are told that the culture in which they live is wasteful, sinful, and devoid of meaning.[14]

Love

A quote from the Koran follows as proof of this point: "And of mankind are some who take (for worship) others besides Allah as rivals (to Allah). They love them as they love Allah. But those who believe, love Allah more (than anything else) . . . (Qur'an 2:265)."[15]

After accusing the West of being a morally bankrupt, criminal, and polytheistic society, hell-bent on wiping Islam off the map, the website next targets capitalism, the system that "has led people to become enslaved to wealth." In what sounds like an Islamist version of Marxist writings, the website condemns capitalism for making money and wealth the absolute forces of benefit. People's souls have "become subservient to the dollar bill in an almost absolute sense, with no acknowledgement of Allah."[16]

Again the Koran is cited: "The Messenger said, 'May the worshipper of Ad-Dinâr [wealth] be wretched. May the worshipper of velvet cloth be wretched. May the worshipper of silk cloth be wretched. May he be wretched and disappointed.'"[17] The 2008 financial crises have been exploited by jihadi websites, with some even adding whole sections to their home pages that portray the crises as yet more evidence of the West's defects.

The ministry of war's indoctrination section aspires to shatter the identity of young Muslims. The jihadi way is freedom, young Muslims are told. The true "universal declaration of freedom of man from servitude" is Islam, which is why jihadism must challenge "all kinds and forms of systems which are based on the concept of the sovereignty of man."[18]

According to the Saved Sect website, Western Muslims must decide whether to continue down this path or choose the jihadi liberation movement. "Democracy and all that emanates from it is retarded and perverse, something that is completely rejected in Islam."[19]

If Muslims reading these unremitting messages begin to view themselves as being part of the problem, then the first stage of jihadi brainwashing, in which there is a radical shift in their own thinking, is nearly complete.

The newly radicalized Muslims must not only alter their worldview, they must also start thinking about how to dedicate their lives to the caliphate. All free time should be spent doing this, as "there is no such concept in Islam called boredom or 'killing time' and this disease affects a large portion of Muslims, male and female."[20]

A long list of activities must immediately disappear from the daily lives of the regular visitors to jihadi websites:

> Listening to music, smoking, cruising, watching TV, running away from responsibilities to go on picnics and holidays, daily socialising with the intention to have fun and kill time, sleeping a lot and chilling out, reading cheap newspapers, magazines, and novels etc., rather than to read more beneficial and serious books such as the Koran, books of *hadith*, Islamic articles etc., playing games, solving crosswords, chatting on the phone for hours, ignoring duties/responsibilities and preferring to rest, slack and be lazy, exceeding one's involvement in sport activities, diverting from the serious, fruitful work to wasting time, playing on the internet for no need, looking for excuses not to do any duties as he is bored with doing them, window shopping and spending hours in the market, going to cinemas and restaurants to eat out, hanging out with friends, joking around and being sarcastic.[21]

A virtual Taliban quickly establishes the dos and don'ts of the modern jihadi warrior.

The Paradise Cult

As they become increasingly alienated from the world, new recruits are taught to despise life and cherish death. The immediate reward for the soldiers of jihad is paradise. That message is drummed into recruits day after day. The allure of paradise allows the online jihadi recruiters to guarantee immediate rewards to those who sign up. Paradise, after all, can be reached instantly.

An e-book written by Sheikh Yusuf al-Uraayi titled "The Ruling on Jihad and its Divisions," which was translated into English by British jihadi ringleader Abu Osama, sings the praises of reaching paradise by dying in an act of jihad. "Whosoever dies and does not fight jihad nor wished himself to fight, dies upon a branch of hypocrisy," the text reads.[22]

The terrifying belief that an act of jihad will result in the reward of paradise is based on an understanding of a quote from the Koran. "Allah traded with the believers, I will give you *jannah* [heaven], if you give me your life and your wealth, they fight in the way of Allah, they kill and are killed. . . . Then rejoice in the bargain which ye have concluded: that is the achievement supreme (English-language Koran 9:111)"[23]

The quote above is taken from an online document called "the Permissibility of Self-Sacrifice Operations," downloaded from a website that espoused jihad in the West. The Muslim nation is under attack, and the twin pillars of Islam, the caliphate and jihad, are missing, the website said.

As an immediate incentive, the lure of jannah has proven its effectiveness. There is no shortage of evidence that this promise has the ability to convince young men to end their own lives for the purpose of jihad, forming one act in a chain of attacks aimed at resurrecting the caliphate.

"We are not targeting for something small . . . we target *jannah* . . . Allah traded with the believers, first with their life, and then their wealth, whether they die by the sword, the gun, or the bomb," the website stated. Being shot on the battlefield or "becoming a bullet for the sake of Allah" are equally valiant. When the time comes, "the martyr will never feel at the time of his death except a pinch."[24]

While many Muslim scholars have ruled that acts of jihad such as suicide bombing are forbidden acts of self-destruction, jihadi websites quickly establish that suicide terrorism is a holy sacrificial act and surround it in a mist of glamour and mysticism. It, like similar acts, is a pinnacle moment of spiritual ecstasy. In online jihadi rhetoric, these acts are called martyrdom operations.

A working definition of martyrdom operations can easily be found among the numerous websites that sanctify jihad. "A specific action performed by the mujahid [holy warrior], with certainty, or least amount of doubt, that it will inflict on the enemy killing and suffering, and that he has certainty or the least amount of doubt that he will reach martyrdom by being killed for the sake of Allah."[25]

While most soldiers are taught to avoid injury to themselves, jihadi recruits are told that coming back unscathed from their mission would be an unmitigated failure. Their harm and demise is necessary to reach heaven. "Either way there is victory, whether he kills or is killed," the website assured.[26]

The rhetoric penetrates deep into the minds of newly brainwashed online recruits. This can be confirmed by a glance at the screen names of members of jihadi chat rooms. Jannah is one gaining popularity.

To increase the bait, fanciful descriptions of the portion of heaven reserved by Allah for the Islamic "martyr" pepper these websites. The virtual caliphate often talks about "the palace for the martyr," a heavenly station where dead jihadis go to enter paradise.[27] Jihadis believe the prophet Muhammad saw the palace during his ascent into heaven and link their descriptions with Muhammad's testimonies.

Allah honors new arrivals at the palace for sacrificing their lives and possessions. They are surrounded by Allah's forgiveness and mercy, reaching the zenith of their existence.

"'And if you are killed or die in the way of Allah, forgiveness and mercy from Allah are far better than all that they amass (of worldly wealths etc).' (3:157)," reads a quote from the Koran, placed next to these fanciful descriptions.[28] Jihadis insist that no one say the martyrs are dead. Although they can no longer be perceived by the living, they are very much alive.

Once inside the palace of the martyr, Allah creates a beautiful replacement body for the dead jihadi's soul, the website goes on, basing its description on an Islamic hadith. The martyr looks down at his old body and the grievers surrounding it. "He then goes towards his wives."[29] These are the infamous seventy-two virgin maidens. But the wives are only one of seven great rewards promised to the jihadi martyr.

The seven rewards are also based on a hadith, and the list appears widely on jihadi websites. The martyr is immediately forgiven for his sins at the "first shedding of his blood."[30] Next he is shown his place in paradise. "He is preserved from the punishment in the grave; he is kept safe from the great terror on the Day of Judgment; he has placed on his head the crown of honor—a ruby of which is better than the world and what it contains—he is married to seventy two wives of the maidens with large dark eyes; and is made intercessor for seventy of his relatives."[31]

Target Defined

> "Fighting the infidels in their homeland is a duty of sufficiency upon all the Muslims, if they [the infidels] do not enter into Islam."[32]
>
> —*Sheikh Yusuf al-Uraayi*

After a sufficient period of exposure to hatred of the West, and indoctrination of a lust for a violent suicide in order to murder infidels, members attracted by the ministry of war's propaganda machine will become ripe for active recruitment. They are now repulsed by a world controlled by infidels and aspire to either reach heaven through an act of bloody terrorism or work through other means to reconstruct the caliphate. The virtual caliphate has prepared its members for war.

5

Online Training Videos

The ministry of war has an array of online training courses aimed at creating terror cells around the world.

One of the most potent means of accomplishing this is to post videos online of holy warriors in the battlefield.

In one video, downloaded in 2005 at a now-defunct British jihad website, young bearded men with guns are seen jumping out of a building as part of a military drill. The terrorist training camp is located in Bosnia, and it is filled with new recruits.

In the video, a Koranic verse can be heard being read slowly and deliberately, as if the narrator were hypnotized or drugged, while the men are seen crawling on the ground with automatic weapons and negotiating difficult structures. A second video from the same training camp in Bosnia features interviews with the recruits.

"My name is Abu Ibrahim," says a masked man in an English accent. He is holding an automatic machine gun and exhibits the telltale signs of jihadi indoctrination. "I am twenty-one years old. I'm a third-year medical student at Birmingham University. And I live in Golders Green, London. I come here, and I see in the West that many brothers say to us that the Muslim nation needs doctors, they need lawyers, they need scientists, they need engineers. And I disagree with that. Because there are enough Muslim doctors. There are enough lawyers, scientists, engineers. But what we lack here are Muslims that are prepared to suffer and sacrifice," Ibrahim tells the camera.[1]

As he continues to speak, a rising rage is discernible in his voice, a product of jihadi brainwashing. "There in Britain I see Muslims . . . every medical student is saying, 'I am studying this for Islam, I study this for the Muslims.' They get their job, they get their surgery. Fifty, sixty, seventy thousand pounds a year, they're earning. And then, no struggle, no sacrifice. Then once a year when Islamic Relief [a charity] comes, they send off a check for a hundred, two hundred pounds, and that's their sacrifice for Islam."[2] Abu Ibrahim is espousing what he has been taught—Muslims who do not set out for jihad are not real Muslims.

"What I feel here when I come here is a sense of satisfaction," he continues, "because every time I'm in Britain, I go to study circles, I go to lectures, I go to talks, and I feel in my heart that something is empty. I watch the TV and tears roll down my face, when I see the Muslims in Bosnia, Muslims in Palestine, Muslims in Kashmir, and then I come here and you feel a sense of satisfaction. You feel that you are fulfilling your duty. You feel that you are doing what the prophet Muhammad and his companions did some fourteen hundred years ago. You feel that you achieved something. People don't know that this is a nice holiday for us, where you meet some of the best people that you will ever meet in your life. People from all over the world . . . and the most important thing . . . you feel a true sense that you achieved something. You come here and in a matter of a few weeks, you free maybe two hundred villages. You see the Serbs, the same people that raped our brothers and sisters, you see their dead bodies lying around in the hundreds. You feel that you achieved something here in a short amount of time."[3]

Muslims from Europe, as well as from around the world, came to Bosnia to fight a jihad against Serbian forces between 1992 and 1995. After Afghanistan, Bosnia provided one of the earliest focal points for the international jihadi movement. And the jihadis were not slow to utilize soldiers' experiences in Bosnia to recruit more soldiers on the Internet. What can be more alluring than seeing highly motivated "brothers" calling on fellow Muslims to join them on the front line? What can be more attractive than going on a "holiday" to a foreign land, to meet like-minded people, and to kill people tagged as anti-Muslim monsters?

"My name is Abu Amman," says a second heavy-set youth on the video. He also clutches a machine gun. "I come from south London. Some brothers back in England, these groups . . . are diseased in the heart. Because what they actually do in England . . . they like to talk. They like to spend money, organizing big conferences, or make a talk in the London Arena, and invite people. And so the people go to these conferences and they sit down, they listen and think, mashallah [praise God], what a beautiful talk. Mashallah, what the brother said was right. And they talk and get worked up." At this point he screams and throws a fist in air. "Allah hu akbar! And then what happens after that? After their talk, they go back home, and they sleep. They carry on watching *Neighbors* [a popular Australian soap opera]. They have their coffee, they drink and eat and stuff their faces! What life is this? Those people talk too much. What do they do with their money? They waste it on these locations to talk, and literature where groups insult each other. True Muslims come with unity to the stage."[4]

By unity, Abu Amman means a machine gun and a suicide bomb belt. When he talks about a "stage," he means an international front of war such as Bosnia, his location at the time of the video.

The stream of new recruits keeps on coming, as the jihadi fighters are swung before the camera and portrayed as model Muslims.

"Some people say that the jihad in Bosnia has been going on for a few years," says a third British Muslim, sitting in a jeep. The man appears more measured and calmer than the first two. But his appearance is deceiving. Like his comrades, this soft-spoken young man is brainwashed and looking for jihad. "And people think, the Muslims . . . they're okay, there's people fighting for them, so they don't need our help anymore. But if you look in the sharia, this is not true. Because the Muslims in the jihad need the help of the rest of the Muslims until the enemy is completely pushed back. Until every single piece of land is taken back. It depends on the amir [leader] of the jihad. And the amir of the jihad here says he needs more help and more equipment. So for people sitting at home and saying, 'They don't need us anymore,' it's not true. Because we need as many people as we can that it takes to push these people back, these Serbs. These are enemy of Allah . . . These people, mujahadeen [holy warriors], come from all over the world. Not just from one Arab country. But many brothers from France and England, from everywhere, from Uganda, from Philippines, everywhere. They come to fight here, not for no money, but for the sake of Allah. For the religion, for Islam. The army couldn't take this mountain, but the mujahadeen did. And this will give guidance to some of the lost people of Bosnia, inshallah [with God's help]."[5]

In August 2005, Swedish Muslims released videos on the Internet of themselves training for jihad in the Swedish countryside. "This was recorded somewhere in

Sweden," says a message on the video in yellow letters, against a backdrop of military-style camouflage colors.[6]

A large explosion is then seen in a heavily wooded area, in what appears to be northern European scenery. A second video released by the group contains images of men with blurred out faces, setting off mock suicide explosives and roadside car bomb attacks. Plumes of white smoke rush out of their devices.

The video tells viewers that they are watching a "demonstration of real high explosives device, that is filled with gas instead of ammoniate nitrate."[7] It goes on to show men standing in a clearing in a forest. They pull on chords attached to devices and set off explosions of white smoke. Simply replace the gas with nitrate, and a suicide bomb squad is ready to attack in Sweden, the video threatens.

In the same video, a red vehicle drives along a forest path before being suddenly engulfed in an explosion of white smoke—an exercise simulating a roadside bomb.

By no means does the ideological brainwashing wane in the ministry of war's training videos. Rather it is intermixed with images of actual recruits training or taking breaks from training for war, and most ominously, images of real fighting.

Scenes of global jihadi attacks serve two purposes: they galvanize the new recruits and fill them with a lust to commit violent acts, while at the same time, they are used as propaganda to convince both Muslims and non-Muslims alike that the soldiers of the soon-to-be-born caliphate are waging a successful campaign of terror.

The distribution of videos showing jihadi attacks is one of the most common features of the virtual caliphate as a whole. Certainly, their value as training videos is immense, as there are not many practical ways to train a suicide bomber, other than by preparing him psychologically to look forward to the end of his life.

For that reason, the virtual caliphate will aim to put out videos of suicide attacks, showing the martyrs in a state of total ecstasy shortly before they set out on their operation, convinced they are shortly due to enter heaven's gates.

In one video released in August 2005 by al Qaeda in Iraq, a young, bearded man reads a lengthy statement pledging allegiance to Osama Bin Laden. He is then seen hugging his friends from the jihad al Qaeda cell, smiling as he bids them farewell. One by one, other armed jihadis come up to hug the soon-to-be martyr. The scene then suddenly shifts to a car moving in the distance. A *nasheed* (Islamic song) plays eerily in the background, praising the merits of holy war, as the vehicle approaches its target: a U.S. military checkpoint. A massive explosion then follows. The blast is replayed in slow motion. As the explosion plays out again and again on the right hand of the screen, an image of the smirking bomber is seen on the left of the screen, smiling, waving, and holding a machine gun. Another martyr has carried out an operation, the virtual caliphate tells its recruits. Follow the footsteps of this man, the video orders.

Another Iraqi al Qaeda video, dated January 12, 2004, begins with the chilling sound of a nasheed, which has a rising and falling siren-like melody, praising the actions of *shaheeds* (martyrs). The singing is repetitive, and the image of computer-generated petals falling from a rose is seen on the screen. Next, a man in his early thirties reads a statement from a piece of paper, with a Koran resting on a machine gun by his side. The man is smiling emphatically and waves mischievously at the camera. He is clearly in a state of barely concealed ecstasy, reminiscent of a drug-induced high. But suddenly the man turns serious. He points at the gun and Koran. He is then seen getting into the driver's seat of a vehicle, laughing and waving at the cameraman.

Inside the car, an unbelievable scene greets the viewer, as the man, armed with a machine gun and still grinning broadly, gently pats an enormous metal-encased explosive device on the passenger's seat. The camera then pans back to reveal that the space between the car's front and back seats are stuffed with additional explosives. With the suicide bomber's enablers filming from a vantage point far behind and chanting repeatedly "Allah hu akbar [God is great]," the tension in the video reaches a peak, as the bomber's vehicle is seen in the distance approaching a major intersection where trucks are passing by. A small, red flare emanates from the bomber's car, before a vast explosion encompasses the entire screen. Cries of "Allah hu akbar" are now at fever pitch and are being shouted with great emotion. An image of the bomber waving from the car is placed at the top right-hand corner of the screen, as the flames of the explosion he caused continue to burn. All the while, a slow, determined nasheed plays in the background, as the explosion is replayed. Viewed enough times, videos like this one form the ultimate brainwashing tool to convert new recruits into willing suicide bombers. These are the ideal training means to program the virtual caliphate's soldiers.

The media producers responsible for distributing these videos have also produced increasingly slick propaganda videos. One video begins with text announcing that the Islamic Media Front had released the footage. It mimics the logo of the

20th Century Fox film corporation. This online video is a chilling compilation of the "top ten" acts of jihad.[8]

"I will instil [*sic*] terror in the hearts of the unbelievers smite ye above their necks and smite all their fingertips off them," the text reads. The justification for the following murderous attacks was based not on the foreign policy of any particular government, but because the targets were "unbelievers."[9]

As the familiar militaristic chanting is heard in the background of the video, an American armored vehicle is blown to pieces by a roadside explosive. The next video shows a car delivering a powerful explosion as an American jeep drives past. The marathon of jihadi attacks continues to roll. The attacks all take place in Iraq. American armored vehicles and soldiers are seen being targeted by various devastating bomb attacks. The jihadi filmmakers even include footage of soldiers dragging their injured or killed comrades away from the scene of the explosions. The "number one" video shows a car driving at full speed into a building, and a subsequent explosion destroying the entire structure. English-language text crawling at the bottom of the video claims twenty American soldiers were killed in that attack. The footage then shows horrific images of the jihadis poking the charred bodies of the U.S. soldiers with a shovel, as the jihadi chanting continues in the background triumphantly. The camera zooms in on the disfigured corpses, emphasizing the images.

A final "bonus" video is at the end, preceded by text addressed to the unbelievers. "We don't care what happens to us, because death for us is a form of victory," the statement reads. "Either way, we are God's soldiers," it adds. "Say: nothing will happen to us except what Allah has decreed for us. He is our protector." The bonus video shows two U.S. soldiers looking out over a balcony, before a sudden explosion goes off nearby. The soldiers are then shot as the jihadis scream, "Allah hu akbar."[10]

The video ends with a request by the jihadis to Allah to "establish our feet firmly, and help us against those that resist faith."[11]

6

The Online Weapons Factory and the Virtual Training Camp

Teaching young soldiers how to make explosives is a major challenge in a physical world filled with police, security forces, and prying eyes and ears. But in the realm of cyberspace, the virtual caliphate's ministry of war has produced hundreds of websites dedicated to weapons training, as well as instruction of bomb assembly skills—the tools jihadis use to tear at the world order they so despise and wish to replace.

Using Microsoft PowerPoint, jihadis have created an online manual to assembling a pipe bomb, complete with diagrams and instructions in Arabic. The file is sent from website to website.

An online video downloaded from a file-storage website—used by jihadis to transfer files anonymously—shows how to assemble, load, and clean an AK-47 rifle. In the background, a jihadi song can he heard, heralding the greatness of Islam.

The online weapons video presents how to maintain the assault rifle and provides lessons in handling shoulder-held rocket launchers and grenades.

"What is the most important equipment which the combatant must have ready?" a message on an Arabic-language al Qaeda affiliated website asks.[1] Sleeper terrorist cells are only one of the ways jihadis can go to war. They can also fight as guerrilla paramilitary units in international battle arenas where jihadis confront "infidel" forces. Training soldiers how to fight in the field is a central task of the ministry of war.

Some content in online jihad training suggests that veteran fighters who survived the war in Iraq and other combat zones have uploaded their experience onto the Internet, gradually building up a virtual library of war training courses. "A combatant operating in the cities requires much less military gear than one who operates in the mountains and forests, because in the city, the fighter will not have to expose himself to others," the online course explains.[2] This is al Qaeda's guerrilla know-how on display.

A jihadi combatant needs to know how to carry his equipment, as mobility is a key to success. "If he can't carry them on his back, he needs to secure them in a safe place where they can be quickly obtained when needed," the guide continues. A jihadi fighter must not make the mistake of depending "on other individuals or units."[3]

Such independence can be achieved by proper preparations, enabling the self-sufficient jihadi fighter to act as a leader and navigator, all the while operating communications and reconnaissance equipment.

The following is a list of what the jihadi fighter in the field will need. Topping this list is a small Koran, "which strengthens the heart and motivates one for fighting." "A light machine gun—which should not impede the performance of combat missions or prevent the carrying of ammunition and bombs. Four magazine clips for the machine gun. No less than 120 storage units of ammunition rounds. Take into consideration that a combat mission may consume a large quantity of ammunition. A targeting lens to be fitted onto the machine gun. Personal pistol for self-defense in case of abandonment of light machine gun, or if you run out of ammunition."[4]

The list also recommends sports shoes, ballistic helmets, and at "at least four grenades." Navigation and communications equipment are important, as a lack of knowledge of local geography "will impede movement and fighting." The guide adds that "there has been much praise for GPS satellite systems, but these do not mean that the map and compass should be dispensed—they will still be needed in case of equipment malfunction." Such advice may well have come from an al Qaeda soldier in Iraq or Afghanistan.[5]

"Solar-powered search lights. Water. A sufficient quantity of food, determined by the military task. Small mattress. Small wooden and small metal hacksaw. Medium sized knife. Personal medical equipment. Video cameras for reconnaissance," the list continues.[6]

Recruits are advised to carry "appropriate quantities of explosives, mines, and detonators. Explosives belts for the martyrdom operations, and deadly rat poison.

Electronic circuits for remote control bombs, or timers. Electric shockers or gas for kidnappings, and handguns for silent assassinations."[7]

A host of tactical battlefield tips are included in the guide, such as how to move from point to point while remaining concealed from enemy helicopters, which are a major problem for jihadi fighters. The guide also calls for good terrain knowledge. Once the area is known, the right equipment can be chosen for the mission. To come unprepared would be going against God's commands, the guide warned. "This is the most important equipment that we feel is needed by a warrior before the battle. The fighter should carry only what he needs for each mission. If he set out an assassination, he only needs to carry poison."[8]

In order for jihadis to acquire the requisite field skills, according to the virtual training camp, they must be able to survive and position themselves using "all forms of camouflage suitable to the field, and attempt to activate all of the unit's firepower during movements."[9]

Describing the basics of hit-and-run guerrilla attacks, the virtual training camp instructed jihadis in "attack and bypass operations, cordon-and-confront, and defending the ambush site," tactics that can likely be identified by American military commanders in Iraq and Afghanistan as being used by the enemy.[10]

Before entering the battlefield, the holy warriors must have their "fighting skills polished, and weapons and equipment ready."[11]

Such guides can be considered a form of "basic training." More advanced training comes in the online form manuals on how to operate sophisticated "smart" weapons, as can be found in the "Technical Mujahid."

The Jamestown Foundation, an American research institute that monitors terrorist activities, has translated the manual into English.[12] The manual takes training for war to the next level, providing guidance on how to operate short-range shoulder-fired missiles, such as the American-made Stinger and the Russian-made Igla missiles.

Abi al-Harith al-Dilaimi has been identified as the author of the smart weapons section. The analysts at Jamestown could barely hide their incredulity over its sophistication. "[He] included many details about the specifications of the missiles, operating manuals and the electronic heat-seeking control systems of the missiles," they wrote in the Jamestown report. "The section is very thorough and even includes pictorial illustrations."[13]

In the weapons manual, al-Dilaimi boasts that al Qaeda has already used some missiles he recommends to down U.S. aircraft. He claims that the Islamic State of Iraq's fighters succeeded in bringing down ten U.S. helicopters in a single month, including the "Apache, Black Hawk, Chinook, and even an F-16 supersonic fighter jet that was shot down in al-Karma area west of Baghdad" in November 2006.[14]

Jihadis are using the Internet to learn how to bring down supersonic aircraft, helicopters, and military cargo planes, the Jamestown report warned, as well as learning how to circumvent missile countermeasures employed by these aircraft, such as heat flares. Al-Dilaimi included detailed information on how to operate the Igla and Stinger missiles. He ended the training with a note, which, much like an advertisement, assures readers that his advice has been tested and proven to work. "'We would like to assert that the mujahideen have proven skillful use of these weaponry by inflicting heavy loses [*sic*] on the colonizing U.S. forces in Iraq and Afghanistan.'"[15]

Training courses of these types can be considered advanced training for jihadis and enable them to operate complex weapons in order to bring down an array of aerial military crafts. Such tactics can be used both on the battlefield in Iraq and by terrorists targeting civilian airports and aircrafts anywhere. One example is the failed attempt to bring down an Israeli passenger jet with a shoulder-launched rocket during an al Qaeda attack in Kenya in 2002.

The Online Bomb Factory

Newly recruited jihadis are trained in how to attack Western troops in Iraq and Afghanistan. Meanwhile, the ministry of war provides resources to help new recruits prepare explosives for use anywhere across the land of war.

One such site, Alamuae, provided a step-by-step guide on how to gather the correct chemicals and put them together in order to produce powerful bombs. Most of the ingredients discussed in the tutorial can be obtained legally in stores or ordered from the Internet.

A message posted on the Alamuae chat site explained how bombs can be assembled based on aluminum nitrate fertilizer.[16] The bomb-making manual instructed jihadis to mix the material with a number of other chemicals.

"Mix them well, and ensure that the nitrate is not moist. Then crush and mix with the other chemicals . . . this can cause an enormous explosion," the site promised.[17]

The bomb-making guides are laced with suggested targets for bombings: "We must impose the harshest blows on the infidels, including the destruction of giant buildings."[18]

Its author falls back on Bin Laden's deputy, Ayman al-Zawahiri, as a motivational figure, instructing jihadis to follow his calls to "focus on the method of the martyrdom operations, make them successful and with the least number of losses for the mujahadeen."[19] The call for small numbers of jihadi casualties in terrorist attacks has been echoed in other areas of the Internet and represents a new trend among online jihadis. It contradicts the sacrificial paradise cult nurtured on so many other jihadi websites.

This web post contained a host of advice for its jihadi audience that went well beyond bomb making; it was aimed at encouraging terror cell formations. Soldiers should use the Internet to "intensify" communications with each other, the online guide said, while working to "maintain the state of terror among the enemy by continuing the threat, and targeting Israeli and American airports . . . continue kidnapping American and Zionist hostages with a focus on abducting journalists and celebrities . . . target the enemy's funds through piracy . . . target the embassies of the countries of blasphemy and apostasy which spy on the Muslims everywhere in the world."[20]

Among the methods of attacks, the post recommended that "remotely controlled car bombs" be used as a "follow up to multiple martyrdom operations." The war plan called for "creativity in the bombings." "Creativity is important in the industry of death and must be used for all means, nothing is unthinkable." Jihadis are encouraged to think outside of the box when plotting to cause the maximum amount of damage possible to their targets. Another section of the guide called for "missile bombardment on embassies" to be considered as an option.[21]

One post taught recruits how to create "toxic smoke." When lit with a fuse, this weapon will create a thick haze covering a hundred meters, the guide claimed. In order to make it, the reader must obtain coal, sulphur, sugar, and other chemicals.[22]

The list of explosive recipes is extensive, as the guide spelled out how to prepare black pepper explosives and how to assemble the correct circuits in order to detonate them.

Specialized Soldiery

As jihadis sift through the ever-expanding material released on the Internet designed to train them, the operators of these websites hope their awareness and ability to vary the weapons will increase.

The sheer magnitude of online help offered on the topic of jihadi combat is well illustrated by the Arabic website, the Manual for Muslim Mujahid.[23]

It contains links to hundreds of other sites that provide training of every conceivable form. The website is divided into four categories: military operations, special weapons, psychological preparation, and physical preparation.

A quick glance at online course titles within the military operations section leaves little to the imagination. Awareness of explosives, the science of bombing, a classification of explosives, the role of oxygen in explosives, conditions affecting explosions, chemical explosives, and a comprehensive course in bomb making are some of the highlights. The list also directs readers to learn "what happens after the explosion."[24]

In the special weapons course, readers are taught how to use Kalashnikovs (AK-47s), the M4 rifle, and handguns. The guide's psychological preparation section discusses "faith and psychological conditioning" and "declaring jihad." The physical guide instructs jihadis on "martial arts" and includes a special "series on preparing for jihad."[25]

In what is one of the more frightening courses provided by the ministry of war, a post provides specific instructions on how best to use explosives to bomb markets and crowded venues. For a successful bombing run, the attacker must enter the market "pretending to be a shopper and carry shopping bags containing the package," the post says. "Choose a place so crowded that no one would notice a bag left behind." Large bombs are no obstacle for an attack on crowded venues. They can be placed inside large cardboard boxes, loaded onto a cart, and pushed through the market as if the bomber "were a goods distributor."[26]

As for bombs with electrical equipment, such as wires, these can be camouflaged in a computer or a printer cardboard package. "Enter the market and buy something such as washing powder. Pretend you are searching for goods inside a shop and put the package aside. In a timely manner, leave the scene quietly and without drawing attention." Another section discusses "operations inside buses and bus stops."[27]

If the bomber boards a bus, he should place his bomb in a briefcase, the manual advises. "But if your plan should be implemented amid a gathering of the enemy inside the station, you can use a large bomb placed inside a travel bag."[28]

If the bomber boards a bus, a large bag is out of the question, "as this will attract attention." But the attacker can place his package in the luggage storage and then get off the bus. "This is a non-martyrdom operation," the guide specifies.[29]

Car Bombs

Much information provided by the ministry of war deals with car bomb preparations. A car bomb can provide a blow many times more powerful than a suicide bomber. According to the manual, car bombs can be used to "storm gatherings of people."[30] The manual says fragments are advisable for increasing the damage caused by the explosion.

The car bomb course goes into great length on where the attack should be carried out. An open market or a bus parking lot are easier targets than a roofed market surrounded by gates. If the jihadi insists on bombing such a market, he should know that car searches are likely and must come prepared with a plan to deceive the guard. The plan is simple: slow down at the entrance as if about to stop, "then suddenly break off at high speed and enter the market, killing the people with your explosives."[31]

Car doors, or the front or back of the vehicle, are the best places to store explosives, the guide says. If driving a taxi, the bomber can place his bomb on the car roof. Car bombs are the weapons of choice for market entrances, stadium exits, and cinema entrances. The jihadi must carry out reconnaissance on this target, learning the route of the people he intends to kill.

As a general rule, the guide states that celebrations, festivals, and any sort of grouping make good targets—a tactic frequently seen in the targeting of Shiite pilgrims and worshippers by al Qaeda bombers in Iraq.

Much time is spent teaching how to avoid drawing attention to the car bomb. The vehicle must be parked legally, and the driver must not act suspiciously in any way in order to blend into his surroundings.

The al Qaeda recruits who attempted to detonate two car bombs in central London on June 29, 2007, failed to heed both of these instructions. One aroused suspicion by crashing his vehicle into garbage bins outside of a nightclub and fleeing the scene, while the other parked his vehicle illegally, resulting in the car being towed away from its intended target.

Martyrdom Belts

Detailed jihadi war tactics seem incomplete without a section on suicide bomb belts, or in jihadi terminology, "martyrdom belts." According to the ministry of war, they should be used in "operations in public places, restaurants, and public service centers."[32]

A lengthy guide provides technical instructions on how to assemble "an al-Qaeda martyrdom belt."[33]

One web page contains the thoughts of a terrorist technician, who comments on the design of his belt with fellow jihadis. "The idea is to stuff manufactured explosive materials into the spaces, as well as electric distribution network and the interface between the right and left sides of the belt," his post reads. "This preserves the explosives until the martyrdom operation is carried out."[34]

The post's author discloses that a number of technicians are working on achieving the best possible design of the explosives belt. No less than three professional bomb makers are working out how to sew the electrics into the bomb belt, which is designed to "distribute electrical wires in such a way that the belt would only be detonated at the time of martyrdom."[35]

The technician also calls on his readers to send in questions and comments, promising to diligently answer each message.

The majority of the tactics discussed at length in this chapter have clearly been put into practice in Iraq, across the country's markets and countless other sites of carnage. Tens of thousands of Iraqis have had their lives brutally ended by these proven attack methods, or as the ministry of war refers to it, by "the industry of death."

It is, however, only a matter of time before jihadis apply these tactics of murder to other places, as they continue to rely on the ministry of war to train and recruit more volunteers.

As mentioned earlier, British police defused a massive car bomb that had crashed into garbage bins outside of a nightclub in the heart of London on June 29, 2007. The car was packed with sixty gallons of gasoline, gas balloons, and nails, and according to London police, it would have killed hundreds of people had it gone off.[36] The Iraqi-style attack was thwarted because of the vehicle's erratic movements, and the terrorist driving the car gave the attack away by crashing his vehicle. Had the driver followed the guide mentioned earlier in this chapter and attempted to carefully blend into the surroundings, carnage would have ensued. What is significant, however, in this failed attack is the exportation of car bomb attacks, very much in the style of al Qaeda's, to the capitals of Western Europe.

The same group, including a doctor and an engineering student, who attempted to bomb the London nightclub also failed in an attempt to carry out a car bomb attack on Glasgow International Airport on June 30, 2007. The terrorists slammed a jeep with gas cylinders into the airport terminal, but the explosives failed to detonate; the would-be bomber escaped, later dying of his wounds. In October 2008, a trial of two of the plotters revealed that the men had used the Internet to plan the attack. "'Bro, inshallah [God willing], I think we are gonna start experiments sometime soon,'" the car bomber, Ahmed, wrote to fellow conspirator, Dr. Bilal Abdullah.[37] An al Qaeda leader in Iraq, Abu Hamza al-Muhajir, went on to claim the Glasgow attack.

Unfortunately, this trend seems likely to continue, and there are no guarantees that future attempts by jihadis in the West will not succeed. The transfer of knowledge, experience, and weapons training—from the battleground in Iraq to Western urban centers—will undoubtedly take place over high-speed Internet connections, the lifeblood of the virtual caliphate's ministry of war.

7

The Ministry of Foreign Affairs

No state can deal with enemies and allies alike without a properly functioning ministry of foreign affairs. The virtual caliphate is not a physical, centralized state and therefore represents a political, ideological, and religious entity of a completely new nature. The virtual ministry of foreign affairs comprises the jihadi websites and online activity that handle relations with other powers and states. In its dealings with other countries, the virtual caliphate follows a model set by the very structure of al Qaeda. On the one hand, messages from the global jihadi movement's leaders to foreign powers reverberate throughout the system; on the other hand, local cells around the world constantly weigh up relations vis-à-vis the states in their own particular regions. Ultimately, the virtual caliphate, like al Qaeda, considers the entire world to be a land of war (Dar al-Harb) and thus can only exist either in a state of open war or in a temporary ceasefire with various states.

The Covenant of Security

For decades, jihadis have used Britain as a base to organize and fund terrorist attacks. Yet Britain was not attacked until the multiple bomb attacks in London on July 7, 2005. Why did al Qaeda's UK branch suddenly decide to turn on its host? The answer lies in a jihadi concept known as the covenant of security, a concept that is openly discussed on British English-language al Qaeda sites.

Six months before the London bombings, Sheikh Omar Bakri Muhammad, quoted in chapter 1, declared that the covenant of security with Britain had ended. But what is this "covenant"?

It is essentially a formula that jihadis use to determine whether their host country should be left alone or attacked. According to a lengthy online post that appeared on the website of the Ahl Sunnah Wal-Jama'ah Muntadaa group, a rehashed version of the banned UK-based al-Muhajiroun, "a *kafir* [infidel] can obtain sanctity either by embracing Islam or by entering into a covenant of security."[1]

Created by the electrician-turned-jihadi-leader Omar Brooks, who had taken the online alias of Abu Baraa (and who has since been arrested by British police for inciting terrorism), the post claimed that according to Islamic law Muslims are permitted to take the lives and wealth of non-Muslims, except for when the infidels have made a pact with the Muslim authorities. A special agreement is needed in which non-Muslims agree to live as second-rate citizens in the caliphate state in order to ensure the security of their lives and properties. Without such an agreement, jihadis such as Brooks believe and preach on the Internet that Muslims are entitled to kill infidels and take their properties.

Brooks stressed, however, that "these are the rules when Islam is dominant. However when the *kuffar* [infidels] are in authority, and we are weak, they look to us as people that have no sanctity, and the only way they will allow you to live with them, is via a covenant—i.e. to have an agreement not to violate the sanctity of each other."[2]

The covenant of security in the modern, caliphate-less era is a modus operandi that allows Muslim minorities to exist in Western infidel countries, in a state of shaky ceasefire, as Islamists prepare for war with non-Muslims and to come to power.

How easy is it for jihadis in their current non-Muslim states to end their self-declared ceasefire? The answer is found in jihadi doctrine, the "covenant of a Muslim living among infidels."

Brooks argued that any state with Muslim minorities "is something that usually would not happen except in unusual circumstances, or in emergencies, it is not normal to live between the infidels."[3] Brooks, born in Jamaica and now in Britain, has lived his entire life in non-Muslim majority states, yet he now views such a situation as "not normal."

According to jihadi ideology, the status of Muslims as minorities in non-Muslim majority states, such as Britain, France, Israel, and Spain, is abnormal and temporary, a situation that will cease to exist when reestablishment of the caliphate takes place.

"Originally it is not allowed to live amongst the infidels, except with a *sharia* permit," Brooks wrote. Quoting Islam's prophet, he declared, "I am free from the one who lives between the *mushrikeen* [polytheists]."[4]

But when Muslim states expel jihadi ringleaders who plot violent revolutions, the whole world becomes a land of war, and Muslims are permitted to live among infidels who will give them the leeway to plot the reemergence of the caliphate.

"For us today where there is no House of Islam, and there is only *taghout* [idol worshipping] rulers oppressing the Muslims everywhere, we are in a position where we are persecuted and oppressed, and it may be necessary to live under covenant in non-Muslim countries," Brooks explained.[5]

After failing to implement Islamic revolutions in Muslim states, jihadis have been forced into exile and have come to live in non-Islamic states. They have developed rules on how to live in their new homes. Indeed, as discussed in chapter 2, Arab-Asian-Muslim states form some of the least hospitable homes for jihadis.

Across the Middle East, in Egypt, Jordan, and other countries, thousands of Islamists languish in prisons and are frequently tortured by security forces, as the targeted regimes quell the Islamic rebellion that threatens them. Hence, so many jihadi leaders flee to safer shores. In Western states, the covenant of security guides jihadis on how to live among infidels and dictates when there is peace between jihadis and non-Muslims, and when there is war.

Unfortunately for the infidel countries, the covenant of security spells out a most shaky and temporary ceasefire, one that seems destined for failure.

According to Brooks, the covenant goes into effect once Muslims enter a new state. In what is probably sound advice for getting past customs, Brooks advises jihadis not to declare jihad on a country when entering it. Rather, jihadis should speak politely and apply for asylum or obtain an entrance visa.

"This is a covenant where they the infidels give you clear verbal or written permission to enter and stay in their country. This is the clearest form of covenant," Brooks stated.[6]

When quizzed by immigration officials, the jihadi must say he has arrived "to study" or "to work" or "for security," but under no condition must he say "to fight."[7]

Once in the country, jihadis agree not to violate the sanctity of the government on the understanding that the government will equally respect the jihadi. "The government represents all the other people however, and so the covenant is applicable to all the people, and so you cannot kill or steal from anybody in that country, while under covenant," Brooks wrote.[8]

If jihadis wish to convince their followers that the covenant is of value, then they must try to anchor it in Islam. Over the past few years, on jihadi chat rooms, jihadi ideologues have developed religious "proof" for the covenant.

In his web posting, Omar Brooks quoted Imam Shafi'i, a cousin of Muhammad, who is considered to be a leading source in Islamic jurisprudence.

"If a Muslim enters a land of war with a covenant of security . . . it is unlawful to take anything from it, Brooks wrote, citing Shafi'i."[9] Brooks falls back on the writings of Imam Abu Muhammad al-Maqdisi, a Jordanian-Palestinian jihadi ideologue who acted as mentor to the late Jordanian al Qaeda commander in Iraq, Abu Musab al-Zarqawi. Maqdisi ruled that Muslims cannot harm or kill infidels in a land of war when a covenant of security is valid.

As the jihadis enter the infidel states, they accept the protection of their new host country and are equally obligated not to harm the state, so long as the state's government is not perceived as persecuting them. If it wants to prevent itself from becoming a target, the government must not curb jihadi activity. The most important questions are, how can the covenant be broken? And what happens after it is declared void?

Leaving the covenant is code for declaring war on the host country and carrying out mass-casualty terrorist attacks within it. There are a few ways to "leave the covenant," according to Brooks: if the covenant, which can be limited to a certain period of time, has expired; if the Muslims have declared that they no longer wish to stay in the land of war state; or if the Muslims have been "betrayed by the ones they have a covenant with." If the covenant has ended, jihadis are supposed to leave the host country and then reenter if they wish to attack.[10]

What counts as betrayal? As far as Omar Bakri Muhammad and Brooks are concerned, when the UK government passed antiterror legislation forbidding incitement to terrorism, the covenant of security had been violated. Another act of betrayal is the "taking of hostages"—arresting jihadi operatives for terrorism offenses. When British police placed al Qaeda figures in jail, such as Abu Qatada, jihadis viewed the arrest and conviction as hostage-taking.

Do Islamists really expect soldiers of jihad to leave Western states and then return to attack? In fact, jihadis have done just that. Throughout the 1990s, thousands of young men left their countries to train in al Qaeda cells in Afghanistan. They then returned to form sleeper cells, waiting to be activated by a command. Many terrorist suspects and would-be terrorists have indeed left their nations and returned. Once a Muslim has reentered a country to fight, the rules change, the covenant of security is invalid, and jihadi open season has commenced, Brooks declared.[11]

In an effort to root the covenant in the Koran, Brooks recited the story of Ka'b ibn Ashraf, a Jewish tribal leader in Arabia beheaded upon the orders of Muhammad. "He was a Jew that would insult and accuse the honor of the Prophet until he [Muhammad] said: 'who can deal with Ka'b? He harms me badly.' Muhammad ibn Maslamah, asked, 'Let me do whatever I like, and I will do it.' The Prophet said: 'you have got it.'"[12]

Maslamah approached Ashraf and claimed he wanted to emulate him and to fight against the Muslims, according to Brooks's online story. Here was an example of a Muslim going undercover among infidels to strike an enemy of Islam. In this case, Brooks deemed deception acceptable and spending time among infidels a legitimate tactic. Maslamah told Ashraf "that he had something to say to him in private."[13] He complimented Ashraf on his perfume, asking his victim to bow his head so he could smell it. Maslamah then produced a knife and decapitated Ashraf.

"Muhammad ibn Maslamah took the head of Ashraf to the Messenger, and the Messenger praised him and his action. He said: 'good doing, good doing.'"[14]

In this account of deception and brutal murder lies the battle plan for al Qaeda sleeper cells hiding out in an infidel state. As Brooks wrote on his website: "There is no doubt here, that Ibn Maslamah acted like an infidel . . . He did so with permission from the Messenger and with the purpose of assassinating Ka'b ibn Ashraf. And the Prophet consented and even praised his action."[15]

A jihadi should thus plant himself within the enemy's society and mimic its conduct while plotting his attacks, Brooks argued. Muhammad has praised such tactics, he claimed. Brooks then cited an Islamic commentator, Imam Shifi'i, as saying that this type of murderous subterfuge guarantees paradise for the jihadi. Shifi'i's words have been reproduced on the British jihadi website centuries after they were first uttered.

"These *kuffar* [infidels] were killed in this kind of assassination. This is the only time and way that you can do so, you cannot act like a kafir, except in war and ONLY in war," Brooks concluded.

A covenant is usually agreed upon by two parties. Brooks claimed that when a jihadi receives an entrance visa or is granted asylum by an infidel state, that country's government has also agreed not to act against jihadi terrorists. But this so-called understanding of an agreement on the state's behalf seems unconvincing. Surprisingly enough, however, some politicians hold the belief that a Western government has secretly signed on to a covenant of security.

According to a high-ranking British politician, there are indeed suspicions that such an agreement did exist between the British government and jihadis in Britain. In a conversation with the author in June 2007 which took place in Tel Aviv, Baroness Caroline Cox, former deputy speaker of the House of Lords, said there are signs that the UK government allowed jihadis into Britain and gave them a free hand to set up base, on the understanding that Britain itself would not be harmed. [16] The fruits of such a policy, if indeed there was one, became apparent on July 7, 2005.

The covenant of security is thus a central foreign policy vehicle that guides relations between local jihadis and their countries of residence. The virtual caliphate's foreign ministry instills the covenant's guidelines into jihadis' minds and also announces when the covenant has ended, declaring war on the host country. The covenant also allows local al Qaeda cell leaders to determine the state of relations between themselves and various states in accordance with their local conditions. The covenant is therefore well suited to al Qaeda's decentralized cell-based structure and grants local commanders a great deal of sway in the global jihadi movement's relations with individual states.

Making Threats, Offering Truces

The ministry of foreign affairs is also activated when al Qaeda's top brass wishes to pass messages along to governments or their citizens. Sometimes the messages are passed to a number of Western states, while others are addressed to specific nations.

In the aftermath of the deadly train bombings in Madrid on March 11, 2004, in which 191 commuters were killed and more than 1,800 injured, the pro-American Spanish prime minister José Maria Aznar lost the general elections and was replaced by socialist José Luis Rodríguez Zapatero.

Before coming to power, Zapatero had vowed to remove Spain's 1,300 soldiers from Iraq and described his country's involvement in the Iraq War as an error. Some observers have claimed that al Qaeda has successfully implemented regime change in Spain.[17]

Was al Qaeda operating according to a plan that appears to have worked perfectly? A document posted online by the Global Islamic Media Front would suggest so, though its credibility has been questioned by experts. Some suggest that the report proves al Qaeda calculated that a bomb attack would ensure Zapatero's victory, although the document's importance and linkage with the Madrid bombing perpetators has been questioned by others.[18]

"'We think the Spanish government will not stand more than two blows, or three at the most, before it will be forced to withdraw [from Iraq] because of the public pressure on it,'" the document read.[19] "'If its forces remain after these blows, the victory of the Socialist Party will be almost guaranteed—and the withdrawal of Spanish forces will be on its campaign manifesto,'" it continued. Commenting on the document in 2004, Adam Dolnik, Director of Research Programs and Senior Fellow of the Centre for Transnational Crime Prevention (CTCP) at the University of Wollongong in Australia, said it was "entirely possible that the perpetrators [of the Madrid bombings] have read this document," but added that "al-Qaeda has be such a fluid concept that almost anyone can claim to speak on its behalf." Dolnik differentiated between anonymously authored online documents, written by top-tier al Qaeda figures, and document that fell into a "grey area" of online writings, "written by unknown authors, inspired by al-Qaeda as an ideology, whether they are actual sworn members of the group or not. So I think we cannot use such documents as clear-cut evidence of involvement of al-Qaeda the group, but they do provide an insight into the dynamically evolving strategic thinking of al-Qaeda the ideology."[20]

Indeed, this grey area is only made possible by the Internet, which allows al Qaeda's ideology to spread to a large number of adherents, who subsequently propagate jihadi ideology and enable al Qaeda's world view to spread around the world.

Whether or not the document is linked to the bombers, al Qaeda's strategy for 'regime change' seemed to have worked, as Spain began to panic and pondered how to withdraw from Iraq as soon as possible.

The al Qaeda document proves that global jihadis, wherever they are situated in the al Qaeda movement, see terrorism as a means to force infidel governments across the land of war to act in jihadis' interests and withdraw their forces from territories earmarked as the future locations of the physical caliphate. Ejecting

Western forces from Iraq lays the groundwork for installing the caliphate in Iraq's Sunni regions.

After the new Spanish prime minister was elected, an al Qaeda–affiliated group operating in Spain publicly instructed its members to "stop all operations within the Spanish territories."[21]

Osama Bin Laden tried—and failed—to exploit the Madrid bombings to repeat an al Qaeda intervention in Western elections in October 2004 by threatening every U.S state that planned to vote for George W. Bush. He hoped a Democratic victory would hasten an American withdrawal from Iraq and remove the last obstacle to setting up the caliphate.

The Madrid bombings also allowed Bin Laden to offer a conditional and temporary truce with Europe. The virtual caliphate's array of jihadi websites has often carried the al Qaeda leadership's offers of truce to Western powers.

In 2005 the late Iraqi al Qaeda leader, Abu Omar al-Baghdadi, who was killed in April 2010 by Iraqi security forces, used the virtual caliphate to offer the Americans an unprecedented "deal": a ceasefire in Iraq in exchange for an evacuation of all U.S. forces from Iraq within a month.[22]

Baghdadi made an audio recording and posted it on a jihadi website. Addressing the American government, he said, "We are offering you the opportunity to withdraw your troops in complete safety, and we are expecting your response within two weeks. We appeal to President George W. Bush to seize this historic opportunity which should allow your troops to pull out in safety."[23]

Bush ignored the offer. Still, a jihadi senior commander used the Internet in order to offer a lull in fighting enemy forces.

Unsurprisingly, the virtual caliphate's foreign ministry is also used to threaten enemies standing in the way of establishing the physical caliphate.

The all-important central media dissemination service of al Qaeda, the Al-Fajr Media Center, is a key transmitter of martyrdom videos, which show actual acts of deadly jihad from the battleground. These videos represent a brutal form of psychological warfare aimed at achieving the intimidation of those standing in the jihadis' way.

Such efforts are assisted by local media groups that create sophisticated propaganda videos to do the bidding for regional al Qaeda forces. A prominent example is the Iraqi Al-Furqan media group, which has been the online mouthpiece of the Islamic State of Iraq.

The workings of al Qaeda's well-oiled Internet propaganda machine were on display when content made on behalf of the Islamic State of Iraq was created by Al-Furqan and distributed worldwide by Al-Fajr.

One of the most interesting threats made on the virtual foreign ministry involves a use of the Global Islamic Media Front (GIMF), another part of al Qaeda's Internet media propagation unit.

In August 2005, GIMF unveiled a profile of the latest al Qaeda recruit, Rakan Bin Williams.[24] Bin Williams is not a real person. Rather, he is a prototype, conjured by al Qaeda, of a Western Christian man who converted to Islam and joined the ranks of the jihad. In the eyes of Western security forces, nothing could be worse than a realization of such a scenario—white Christian European converts preparing for jihad and operating out of sight of intelligence radars, practically undetectable.

GIMF plays on such fears and claims al Qaeda is busy recruiting white terrorists. "'Al Qaeda's new soldiers were born in Europe of European and Christian parents. They studied in your schools. They prayed in your churches and attended Sunday mass. They drank alcohol, ate pork and oppressed Muslims, but al Qaeda has embraced them so they have converted to Islam in secret and absorbed the philosophy of al Qaeda and swore to take up arms after their brothers,'" the online message read.[25]

Western governments should be very afraid, GIMF warned, because white terrorists "'are currently roaming the streets of Europe and the United States planning and observing in preparation for upcoming attacks.'"[26]

If Rakan Bin Williams, a white British male, boards a train with a suicide bomb belt or navigates a car packed with explosives near a populated city center, he is much more likely to succeed. In reality, a number of individuals have already joined al Qaeda, such as the American al Qaeda member John Walker. Security forces can only hope that such a phenomenon remains confined to a few isolated incidents and the imagination of al Qaeda's propagandists.

"'You will not be able to find any solution because our next soldier cannot be put under surveillance or restrict his movement or arrest him,'" GIMF continued.[27]

In this case, the ministry of foreign affairs is being used to deliver a threat to instill fear and terror in Western governments and citizens. The threat is not completely imaginary. Over the years, videos of just such a person—a Western convert to al Qaeda—have been posted repeatedly by al Qaeda's main media production arm, As-Sahab.

As-Sahab has produced many slick jihadi videos and plays a key role in al Qaeda's propaganda department. Its first video was released in 2001 and featured Adam Yahiye Gadahn, a California native whose original name was Adam Pearlman.[28]

The grandson of a prominent Jewish doctor, Adam was once a death-metal music fanatic before becoming a jihad fanatic.

He was recruited into radical Islamist circles at an Orange County mosque and reportedly traveled to Afghanistan for combat training. According to *LA Weekly*, he has been linked to the "millennium plot" to attack Los Angeles International Airport on New Year's Day 2000 and is on the FBI's list of most wanted terrorists.

LA Weekly asked a veteran terrorism expert to explain why As-Sahab was so keen to post videos of Gadahn. "Here's a guy who can talk to Americans in English. He can indicate that he knows us and our culture. . . . The national media has brushed this videotape aside, but it has all the markings of bin Laden—the graphics, the cutaways, the level of sophistication—only in English. He's in the inner circle of the al Qaeda hierarchy, or he wouldn't have access to these things. This is very clever psy-ops right out of the al Qaeda front office," the expert said.[29]

Laying Claim to Europe

Another key usage of the virtual foreign ministry can be found in the form of a surprising territorial claim.

An online message by GIMF discussed a 2005 al Qaeda bombing spree in Turkey and Morocco. The bombings had an astounding purpose, according to GIMF. They were aimed at undermining "'the border between Europe and the Muslim world, east and west, so let this serve as a lesson to the entire west; we have arrived at your borders and no one will be able to stop us.'"[30]

As noted in earlier chapters, a staple of jihadi ideology is based on the belief that Muslims have a God-given duty to conquer the world and convert it into an enormous caliphate.

This kind of rhetoric is also backed up with online tales recounting glorious medieval memories of the Islamic conquest of Spain and the failed attempt to take France. In April 2007, as French citizens went to the polls to select a president, jihadi members of an al Qaeda online forum exchanged messages discussing their aspiration to "reinvade France (and convert it into) an Islamic country."[31]

The online discussion appeared as Spanish security forces warned that both Spain and France were targets of al Qaeda terror plots.

A post that appeared on the al-Firdaws jihadi forum, submitted by a user named Faisal al-Baghdadi, contained a lengthy historical account of "the second stop of the Islamic conquest of Europe, France, after Andalusia, Spain.[32]

The post took a nostalgic look at the battle of Tours in 732, in which Muslim forces, commanded by Rahman al-Ghafiqi, invaded a portion of France before being repelled by the Frankish general Charles Martel ("the hammer"), and forced to retreat. The battle stemmed the medieval Islamic advance on Europe.

Writing about the battle, the post's author notes that Ghafiqi's Islamic army was left with "many martyrs," including the acclaimed general himself.

"We ask that Allah sends us a genuine Rahman al-Ghafiqi, to finish what he started in Europe, and conquer the Vatican as promised in our beautiful Islamic verses," the post concluded.[33]

"Allah bless the writer and carrier of the message which recalls the days of glory and honor of Islam," another user responded.[34]

This conversation highlights a key use of the foreign affairs section of the virtual caliphate—to remind Muslims of historic epochs of Islamic conquest and sovereignty over lands now in infidel hands.

In April 2006, MEMRI, the Middle East Media Research Institute, examined the children's section of the Muslim Brotherhood website. "The 'My Great Homeland' section depicts Seville and Andalusia as part of the Muslim homeland, along with Egypt, Damascus, the Al-Aqsa mosque [in Jerusalem], Istanbul, Bosnia-Herzegovina, and the Maldives," MEMRI stated. [35]

The Muslim Brotherhood website gleefully reported that 700,000 Muslims now live in Spain, 200,000 of whom are Spanish-born citizens. The purpose of reciting these figures is to contribute to the sense that Muslims are "taking back Spain." Madrid, Barcelona, and Valencia are Muslim population centers, and Spain boasts no less than 300 mosques, the website said.[36]

Al Qaeda had issued several fatwas prior to the Madrid bombings, calling for the "liberation of Andalusia." For al Qaeda, influencing the outcome of Spanish elections is merely the first step to retrieving control of Spain.

Linking Jihadi Fronts

What do Israel, Spain, Kashmir, Thailand, Chechnya/Russia, and Somalia have in common? They have all been marked out as central fronts for the jihad. It takes the virtual caliphate's foreign ministry to focus jihadis' minds on all of them simultaneously and to present them as a unified Islamic front—as areas that should be conquered and placed under the flag of Allah.

A brief examination of online messages addressing jihadi conflict zones reveals a concerted effort to use one location to remind Muslims of other front lines.

In January 2006, UK jihadis operating under the name the Followers of Ahl Us-Sunnah wal Jamma called for a demonstration outside of the Israeli embassy in London. The rally was aimed at showing support for the intensification of jihad against the enemies of Allah, according to an online leaflet.[37]

The rallying call for the demonstration was one for verbal, financial, and physical support to the holy warriors attacking "the fascist entity called Israel so that it can be destroyed once and for all" and replaced with an entity that would allow "the Muslims to implement Islamic law." Jihadis must not lose hope and "continue the good work of removing the cancer of Israel from the body of the Ummah of the Messenger Muhammad." The battle against Israel is just one in a series of frontline struggles between truth and falsehood, Islam and disbelief, Muslims and infidels, the message continued.[38]

The Followers used their websites to attack India, Russia, and other nations in similar ways and, as described in chapter 5, have spent decades sending young soldiers to the front lines around the world. All of these fronts are a single trench in which the soldiers of Allah gather.

The virtual foreign ministry routinely alternates the spotlight on various regions around the world, which is evident in a story posted on Islamic Awakening about Bilal, one of the many martyrs.[39]

Bilal first picked up a gun for jihad in 1995 when he went to Bosnia, where he fought for six months, the website tells its readers. He then attempted—and failed—to travel to Chechnya to join the jihad there.

After a brief detour in Turkey, where he was supposed to get married, Bilal instead traveled to Ogadeen, East Africa. Always eager to fight, Bilal made his way to Kosovo to fight for the Muslims there, but the war ended one month later. It was only in August 1999 that Bilal made his way to Chechnya to take on the infidel Russian forces attacking Muslims. After taking part in a number of operations, Bilal and his fellow fighters, who had come to support the Chechen guerrilla forces, found themselves facing a Russian invasion. Bilal fought battles in Argun and Grozny, Chechnya's capital. He was a dutiful jihadi soldier, preparing food for the mujahideen in his group during Ramadan. "During the fighting he was distinguished for his bravery," the website points out.[40]

Bilal's movements symbolize the international focus of the virtual caliphate. Islamic Awakening proudly recounts the tale of Bilal's martyrdom. "After seeing a dream in which he was married, he made his intention to marry a Chechen, but Shahaadah [martyrdom] was destined for him instead." Bilal sustained injuries during a withdrawal from Grozny in an outlying village, where his room absorbed a direct hit from a Russian artillery shell. He subsequently died of his injuries in a Chechen village. "Allah accept your martyrdom O Bilal and marry you to the 72 Paradise Maidens as you saw in your dream."[41]

Bilal fought in several arenas separated by thousands of miles. All of them part of one struggle, *Islamic Awakening* says.

This international focus pops up repeatedly. The al-Jihaad blog, for example, claims to contain horror stories of terrorism by "occupation forces in Iraq, Palestine, Afghanistan, Chechnya, and Kashmir."[42]

The Malaysian Islamic-World.net website attempts to draw its readers' attention to several Islamic fronts at once. A message on the website expresses "deep sympathy for our brothers and sisters" in Somalia, Lebanon, Palestine and Iraq, where Muslims are being denied their right to set up the caliphate and "are being subjected to an unending nightmare of terror, torture, violence, and death."[43] No distinction is drawn between the various areas named in the message—all are part of a single conflict.

8
Uploading the Virtual Caliphate

The ministries of war and foreign affairs are two of the most vital centers of activity driving the virtual caliphate forward. There are other discernible formations of jihadi web activities that can be classed into ministries and are no less interesting and relevant (these ministries will be examined later in the book). At this stage, however, it is important to address an issue that goes directly to the core of the virtual caliphate's existence.

As stated in chapter 1, the online jihadi presence is pervasive because of the lack of a physical space for Islamists to construct their utopia, the caliphate. Although the virtual caliphate defies notions of statehood and culture based on a concentration of people in one geographic location, in the eyes of the jihadis, the online kingdom they have constructed is no more than a temporary, albeit vast, shelter housing the true, physical caliphate, for which the jihad is being waged.

Al Qaeda hopes to one day soon "upload" the virtual caliphate and turn it into a physical state. The questions are, where can such a state be formed? Which areas has al Qaeda eyed? The answers are surprising.

Gaza Strip

The Gaza Strip is a small territory situated on the Mediterranean coast, bordering Israel to the east and north and Egypt to the south. Over one million Palestinians live there, and a recent military coup carried out by Hamas in 2007 now means that a violent offshoot of the Muslim Brotherhood has formed Gaza's government. Hamas rid Gaza of the secular Fatah and thereby cleared the path for establishing sharia law in Gaza—something it has yet to do formally. In the meantime, two Palestinian states are unofficially in existence: the Hamas regime in Gaza and the Fatah regime in the West Bank, with each polity having separate governments and armed forces, and each extremely hostile to the other.

Founded by Palestinian Muslim Brothers who joined the Brotherhood while studying in Egypt, Hamas is in no hurry to establish a caliphate in Gaza. Some observers, including embittered al Qaeda members, say Hamas has been infected with a nationalist bug, leading it to fuse Islamism and Palestinian nationalism together and to distance itself from the global jihadi movement. If Hamas's jihadi detractors are right, Hamas may never declare a caliphate, as such a state would look upon any separate Palestinian national identity with scorn. If, however, Hamas one day finds itself willing to part with nationalism, it may yet declare a caliphate after it feels that society has been sufficiently Islamasized and that the caliphate is a viable option. First, however, Hamas will try to take over the West Bank.

In addition, Hamas's recent alliance with Shiite Iran has caused tensions with Sunni al Qaeda, which accuses Hamas of straying from its Sunni roots. Hamas, however, views the intensive cooperation with Tehran as a convenient partnership because it is one of the the few Middle Eastern state willing to openly and fully support Hamas, militarily, financially, and rhetorically.

Hamas's failure to declare an Islamic political entity in Gaza has already spurred complaints by members of the al-Firdaws jihadi Internet forum. "When Hamas took over Gaza, we eagerly anticipated their announcement of the establishment of an Islamic emirate, as was the case in Afghanistan and in Somalia," a Palestinian forum user, who described himself as affiliated with al Qaeda, said. "But this did not happen."[1]

While Gaza cannot be ruled out as a future caliphate start-up point, local circumstances and the current state of Hamas's worldview seem to make such a development unlikely for the time being. Still, the jihadi web forums are receiving messages of protests demanding the creation of an Islamic emirate in Gaza, composed by Palestinians who claim they stand with al Qaeda, not Hamas.

Afghanistan

Scene of the closest attempt yet to rebuild the caliphate, Afghanistan is also a potential caliphate zone. Somewhat preemptively, the surviving elements of the Taliban and al Qaeda, who have now regrouped and are launching guerrilla attacks on Western forces in an effort to destroy the nascent Western-backed Afghani state, have declared online that they have established an Islamic emirate in Afghanistan.[2]

For the sake of clarification, an Islamic emirate is not a full-fledged caliphate; rather, the term is used to describe some form of a jihadi republic that hopes to soon be recognized as a full-fledged caliphate. In Afghanistan's case, jihadis had built a website called the Islamic Emirate, which was mainly used to report on jihad attacks on NATO forces until the site was shut down. A number of attempts have been made to revive the website; each so far has failed.

The declaration of an Islamic emirate at this stage represents the aspirations of al Qaeda's ongoing battle to drive out Western forces and destroy the government of President Hamid Karzai. With determined U.S. and Western commitments to repel the Taliban, Afghanistan, like Gaza, seems a distant candidate for the spot where the caliphate will be reborn. Afghanistan is a volatile land, however, and it has already hosted the most recent bid for jihadi sovereignty: the Taliban. It cannot be ruled out as a future caliphate country.

Until it was shut down, the Islamic Emirate website focused most of its content on gleeful reporting of Taliban attacks on NATO forces. The website's home page was divided into dates, and underneath them, each attack was detailed. "November 19, 2006: Five mortars were fired on Sarobi district (police) headquarters. In an attack, two US invader soldiers were killed in Kunar. Mortars were fired on an invader convoy in Arozgan," read a typical post on the website.[3] For additional details, the reader could click on the attack's description.

"November 17, 2006: In an explosion, a large number of soldiers from the Afghan mercenary army were killed in Farah. Two supply vehicles of US troops were torched in Zabul. Two Afghan military vehicles were destroyed in Ghazni."[4]

Occasionally, the website would mock statements made by the Western-supported Afghan president and challenge the Afghan government's legitimacy. But the website's focus on listing daily military assaults underlines the stage at which the so-called emirate is—fighting to be born. The Taliban has successfully regrouped in the lawless tribal border areas between Afghanistan and Pakistan, and nine years after the U.S.-led invasion of Afghanistan, it shows no sign of weakening, let alone disappearing.

Pakistan

Pakistan, the only nuclear-armed Muslim country, has suffered growing instability due to a serious internal Islamist challenge and the newly empowered jihadi presence in the Pakistan-Afghanistan border region. In 2008, Pakistan increasingly felt the efforts of jihadis to implement regime change in the country, a situation made worse by the fact that jihadis have infiltrated the country's military and the ISI (Inter-Services Intelligence). On September 20, 2008, a truck bomb laden with six hundred kilograms of explosives slammed into the gates of the prestigious Islamabad Marriott Hotel, a hub for Westerners and diplomats. Fifty-five people, including the Czech ambassador to Pakistan, were killed, and much of the hotel was left in ruins. The bombing came amid a flurry of jihadi Internet chatter calling for Pakistan to be the next seat of the re-established caliphate.

"'It's time for you to put aside tribal, ethnic and territorial differences and petty worldly disputes not just for now but forever and unite to restore the glories of your forefathers and hasten, Allah willing, the defeat of the Zionist-crusader enemy and the establishment of the Islamic state, the Ummah, the so eagerly anticipated,'" said American al Qaeda member Adam Gadahn in a video message posted days after the Marriott bombing.[5]

The entire Indian subcontinent has been affected by the jihadi resurgence in the region. In the summer and autumn of 2008, India suffered a spate of bomb attacks in markets and crowded venues across the country as Indian police scrambled to apprehend the perpetrators. In his message, released by the Sahab al Qaeda media production company, Gadahn also called for "'victory in Kashmir,'" adding, "'It is the liberation of the jihad there from this interference which, Allah willing, will be the first step towards victory over the Hindu occupiers of that Islam land.'"[6] From November 26 to November 29, 2008, Mumbai was targeted by a massive coordinated jihadi attack by Pakistan-based extremists, which claimed the lives of 173 people.

Dr. Ely Karmon, an expert on Islamist movements and their drive to obtain weapons of mass destruction, says radical Pakistani Islamists have set the goal of gaining access to Pakistan's estimated eighty to ninety nuclear bombs, an arsenal they call the Islamic Bomb.

Throw into the mix the fact that two leading Pakistani scientists have been found to cooperate with al Qaeda members, and the proliferation of nuclear weapons technology via black market established by Pakistani scientist Abdul Qadeer Khan, and one can see why Pakistan's instability is holding the attention of Western governments.

Iraq

Although it is has shifted its focus to Pakistan and Afghanistan (again), al Qaeda still has many of its chips stacked on Iraq, or more accurately, the Sunni region of Iraq, as the area from which the caliphate will rise. Jihadis hope the caliphate will then spread out around the Middle East, toppling other Sunni states in a tsunami-like wave of Islamic revolution, creating a worldwide caliphate.

As mentioned in chapter 2, Islamists have already taken the step of declaring the Islamic State of Iraq. An array of websites now embodies that state online.

Much of the Islamic State of Iraq's web presence resembles that of the Afghani Emirate. Several times a day, the actions of the state's jihadi army are flashed around the world on these websites. On the infamous al-Firdaws website, a special section was created and tasked with reporting on the dozens of daily attacks carried out by the Islamic State in 2007 and 2008. These years were the peak of jihadi violence in Iraq, before the U.S. was able to largely regain control of Iraq's security situation through a combination of a surge in combat troops and a hearts-and-minds campaign directed at Iraq's Sunni tribal chiefs. Although greatly damaged, al Qaeda cells today still work relentlessly to terrorize Iraqis in order for them to stop supporting the Western-backed Iraqi state, and to replace Iraq with a newly established caliphate.

One section of a jihadi website, called the Ministry of Information of the Islamic State of Iraq, reports on the progress of its "Islamic Army" and issues statements to Iraqi Sunnis in an effort to recruit them, as well as threats to Iraqi Shiites and Kurds.

In an "Appeal to Sunnis in Iraq," dated December 18, 2006, the Islamic State asked Iraqi-Sunni scientists to join the war effort and share their scientific expertise to help establish the caliphate.[7] By describing their organization as a state, jihadis in Iraq hope to imbue a sense that they have built an Iraqi shadow jihadi state. The shadow state's organizers not only call for soldiers and car bombers, but also for technical experts and scientists.

Likewise, the Caliphate Voice Channel website has been used to attack the legitimacy of the official Iraqi state. Iraqi Prime Minister Nouri Maliki (who in the eyes of al Qaeda is a Shiite, an infidel, and an agent of Iran) is described as "the occupation-appointed prime minister."[8]

Any communal leaders in Iraq who meet and cooperate with Maliki "are spineless puppets, acting upon the direct order of the green zone occupiers [the Americans]." That was the view of the "true" sons and sheikhs of the "jihadi and steadfast" al-Anbar province, the Caliphate Voice Channel website said, in an attempt to rob the Iraqi government, and all of Iraq's tribal leaders who have allied with it, of any semblance of legitimacy.[9]

The *ummah* (Islamic nation) knows the true situation in Iraq, the Caliphate Voice Channel declared. "It is the final conquer of the unbelievers and the complete disintegration of the American Crusade project."[10] Victory is just around the corner for the jihadis in Iraq, and they will soon celebrate in joy as the infidels are vanquished, the website assured.

"June 30, 2007/Islamic state of Iraq. Nine soldiers finished off, control of the guard of the idoltarors [sic] ended," a news flash on the al-Firdaws site said. "God has enabled soldiers of the Islamic State to attack, using light and medium weapons, and RPG rockets," the Islamic Army reported proudly.[11]

"July 2, 2007/Islamic state of Iraq. Blessed martyrdom operation on joint checkpoint in town of Fallujah against apostates. Launched by brother Kareem, from the youth of the Martyrs Battalion. His car collided with a checkpoint of the army and police . . . the operation resulted in the death of the blessed [martyr] and dozens wounded. God is great," read another jihad report.[12]

Every day, dozens upon dozens of such reports from the Islamic State of Iraq are filed on jihadi websites. The ongoing war in Iraq and casualty toll represent a battle to reestablish the first potentially viable caliphate since the 1920s. Now that U.S. forces have mostly departed from Iraq, there is every reason to believe jihadis will intensify efforts to establish the caliphate on the Sunni regions of central Iraq. Hemmed in by the Shiite south and the Kurdish north, the potential caliphate could find itself under attack as soon it is born. But the thought of such a confrontation is relished by certain elements of al Qaeda, eager to target Shiites. Certainly such a development would mean the demise of the now-unified Iraqi state.

"Praise be to Allah, prayer and peace on our Prophet Muhammad, his family and companions," a message from the Islamic State of Iraq on the al-Hanein jihadi website began.[13]

The message went on to accuse Fallujah's police force and "loyalists of the so-called Save the Anbar organization, founded by Crusaders," of cold-blooded murder of jihadi prisoners, warning that "this will not go unpunished."[14]

The post divulged recent intelligence received by Iraqi jihadis: police are executing prisoners of the Islamic State of Iraq organization after taking them to remote areas "under the pretext of transporting prisoners to jail."[15]

"After an investigation, as well as the people of the area who found corpses and saw police cars received the bodies in the area in question (The Emirate of al-Fallujah), we say to our prisoners that God will offer salvation shortly . . . we will outmanoeuvre the rancorous Shiites, Zionists and Crusaders."[16]

This message contains a number of important clues as to jihadis' progress in founding the caliphate in Iraq. It describes Fallujah as an emirate, a sign of how dominant al Qaeda felt at the time of this Internet message. Fallujah—in the heart of the Sunni Triangle and at the core of al Qaeda's forces—could well serve as the reestablished caliphate's first capital.

The statement's call for revenge against alleged police killings of Islamic State soldiers also underlines the Islamic State's aspiration to undermine official Iraq's security forces. Finally, the Islamic State has identified "Shiites" (described as "rancorous"), "Zionists and Crusaders" as the enemy, echoing global al Qaeda rhetoric, which argues the existence of a Christian-Jewish plot to destroy Islam. The addition of Shiites to that list is a recent development and signals the escalation of the centuries-old Shiite-Sunni conflict in Iraq, one that has the potential to descend into an all-out war for control over Iraq.

Al Qaeda has done its best to ignite this sectarian conflict, with repeated bombings of Shiite holy shrines and massacres of Shiite civilians. They have hoped that Shiites will respond in kind—a bait some Shiite militias have taken, although a number of influential Shiite Iraqi leaders have seen through the plot and have counseled restraint. Such restraint would sabotage al Qaeda's efforts to make the situation on the ground in Iraq intolerable, prompting the collapse of the current Iraqi state and clearing the path for a caliphate to stand on. As U.S. forces prepare to leave Iraq, jihadis are preparing to once again escalate the war for an Iraqi caliphate.

The danger that such a state would pose to world security should be clear from the tentacles of terrorism already sent out by the Islamic State of Iraq group. In the early stage of their investigation into the failed London car bombings, British security forces suggested that al Qaeda in Iraq, and its former leader, Zarqawi, instigated the plot to sow mass carnage across Britain with Iraqi-style coordinated car bombings.

The sheer determination of al Qaeda forces operating in Iraq to reestablish a caliphate, driven by blind religious-ideological fervour and the use of the virtual caliphate, certainly make Iraq, or the Land of the Two Rivers in the language of jihadis, a region that could potentially host the establishment of a new, physical caliphate.

Britain

How could a country with an estimated two million Muslim citizens and fifty-eight million non-Muslims be a potential candidate for the caliphate? Those demographics do not concern the British branch of al Qaeda, which constantly uses the virtual caliphate to discuss plans on how to set up the caliphate on the British Isles. Its members hope that a mixture of missionizing and jihad will achieve a miraculous wave of conversions to Islam, after Britons see the divine justice they say is prevalent in Islam.

A lively online audio and text conversation ensues within a chat room called "Islamic State for Britain" on the Paltalk chat network. Dozens of users are in the room, zealously discussing the best ways to make the United Kingdom an Islamic caliphate.

The topic of the chat is how to "rise against the rulers," and the preacher is Abu Baraa, the Jamaican convert to Islam who became a Salafi jihad preacher. Abu Baraa explains to his listeners that even if U.S. and British troops left Muslim lands, the jihad must continue, because the "puppet governments" installed in Afghanistan and Iraq represent continued "occupation."[17]

"The Muslim lands are still occupied. Just because they left the land doesn't mean their puppets are not occupying the land," he says. "The fighting will not stop," he continues, heaping praise on the "mujahadeen who don't compromise and fight the jihad."[18]

Baraa then takes his speech one step further by demanding that Islamic law be applied in Britain. "You've got the British parliament, where they sit and discuss how to contravene Allah's deen [law]," Abu Baraa declares with a tone of outrage.[19]

The British parliament is guilty of sins such as debating the legal drinking age, he laments, even though Allah has forbidden the consumption of alcohol. The fact that Britain is not a Muslim state is Baraa's main bone of contention.

"Allah said alcohol is *haram* (forbidden). How can you sit there and discuss, should we make it legal or not?" With rising anger, Baraa continues, "They put it to a vote! They vote on whether an 18 year-old or a 16-year old can drink. A 16 year-old or a 14 year-old. How can you discuss this in parliament?! It is impossible to discuss things with the infidel."[20]

"Parliament even thinking about this [legal drinking age] is *haram*. This is Kuffar-Akhbar (typical action of non-believers)," Abu Baraa cries out.[21] He then called for Islam to be implemented into the British parliament.

In the eyes of UK jihadis, the first step to converting Britain into a caliphate involves raising awareness among British-Muslims that participation in the infidel British state processes is illegal, as it involves recognizing the legitimacy of a non-caliphate state system.

One of the first targets of this campaign was the Respect Party, a Far Left political party in Britain that had begun to attract a great deal of Muslim votes. Founded by George Galloway in 2004, the party rests on an alliance between the Socialist Worker's Party (SWP) and the Muslim Brotherhood's UK branch, the Muslim Association of Britain (MAB). Unlike al Qaeda, the Muslim Brotherhood believes Muslims must first be made sufficiently religious before beginning to construct the caliphate. But al Qaeda dismisses that view as naïve, calling for immediate jihad for the creation of the caliphate.

In order to stress their message that taking part in the British political system is forbidden, UK jihadis targeted one of the most Muslim-friendly political parties in Britain. "The Respect Party is kafir [infidel] organisation which, like every other political party, believes that sovereignty belongs to man and not Allah," an online statement read on the website of the Saved Sect group, a renamed al-Muhajiroun faction.[22]

Respect's sin is to recognize the British state and lure Muslims into believing that democratic participation, rather than jihad, can bring change.

"They have full 'respect' for nightclubs, nudism, alcohol, pornography, homosexuality, fornication, adultery, interest, free-mixing, music, gambling and freedom to insult the *sharia* under the pretext of freedom of speech," the message continued.[23]

The Saved Sect website leveled charge after charge at the Respect Party in the statement. The Respect Party was guilty of employing Muslim grassroots activists to heavily leaflet London's Muslim neighborhoods, thereby attempting to involve British Muslims in the electoral process. The Saved Sect considered such acts as sins, since recognition of a secular political system meant betraying a divinely mandated order. In response, the Saved Sect handed out its own leaflets to Muslims living in the same areas. One leaflet distributed by Saved Sect members carried the following message:

> Dear voter… we were extremely shocked that "Muslims" could distribute such an item [leaflets printed by the Respect Party]. George Galloway himself clearly affirmed that he will represent you and your vote; so how is it that "Muslims" could vote for such a person, knowing very well that he is going to make laws and play the role of God?[24]

Quoting an infamous hadith, the Saved Sect attempted to back up their radical views with an Islamic proof, throwing their own interpretations in brackets. "Allah says in the Koran: 'Oh you who believe, do not take the Jews and the Christians (the non-Muslims) as your friends (or representatives) for they are friends (and representative) of one another. And whosoever allies with them (e.g. by voting or taking sides with them), then surely he is one of them . . . ' (English Koran 5: 51)."[25]

Placing the word "Muslims" in quotation marks represents a challenge to the legitimacy of all Muslims who not only vote in British elections, but who also cast their ballot for a Far Left party that claims to represent their interests. According to the Islamists, nothing is legitimate other than the destruction of the British state and its replacement with the caliphate. Until that happens, Muslims must refrain from all transactions that grant recognition to the noncaliphate state in which they live.

Referring to the cult of paradise and its promised rewards, the statement's authors argued that the position of secular politicians in the Islamic afterlife looks bleak. Anyone who is not a believing Muslim is destined for hell, they alleged, and that includes Muslims who follow non-Muslim secular politicians. "Do these hypocrites really want a *kafir*, such as George Galloway, to represent them in the hereafter? Yes they do, and may Allah put them with him on the Day of Judgment!"[26]

UK political parties claiming to be guided by a desire to represent Muslims will not help "our brothers and sisters in Iraq and Palestine, yet they are the very same ones who condemn the retaliation and operations of the *Mujahadeen*, labelling them as extremists and terrorists!"[27]

Infidel politicians, no matter how friendly, are the descendants of British imperialists who raped and murdered Muslim women and children. Today, the apple has not fallen far from their tree, and "they have still not repented for their evil actions," the jihadis said.[28]

The Saved Sect issued a warning to British Muslims to not be fooled by "these evil pretenders" and their promises of support on Islamic causes. Muslims in Palestine and Iraq are not helped by voting for the Respect Party, the Saved Sect said. Voting for any party contravenes Allah's command "'[not to] associate anything (in worship) with me. But whoever disbelieved after this, they are the *Faasiqoon* (rebellious, disobedient to Allah).' (English Koran 24: 55)."[29]

The last quote from the Koran is used to make an explicit promise to Muslims; if they refrain from taking part in British non-Muslim political processes, they will be rewarded with a caliphate. Vote today, become infidel tomorrow, "if not sooner," the message ended.[30]

Despite being a minority in Britain, the followers of Ahl ul-Sunnah wal-Jamaa'ah say they are unwilling to accept the rule of non-Muslims. "Hence, we hereby reject the deception and trickery of these nations and their filthy, rotten, democratic way of life for we have Islam which is the only divine unique and supreme way of life where the sovereignty is to Allah alone."[31]

Assuming that jihadis conquer the hearts and minds of their fellow British Muslims—a scenario which is unlikely to ever emerge—and convince them that participating in noncaliphate state processes would lead them directly to the flames of hell, how do Islamists plan to implement stage two of their plan, taking power in the United Kingdom? As always, jihadis have a plan of action on the Internet. The al-Ghurabaa website lists three ways "in which a state or country can become Dar al Islam."[32] The first way to turn a country into a caliphate is to have the majority of the state's citizens convert to Islam and voluntarily choose to have Islamic laws as their constitution. The second way in a Muslim-majority state is if an Islamist organization carries out a violent coup and installs a caliphate regime, the strategy jihadis pursed for decades. And the last path, an existing caliphate expands its borders via jihad and swallows up non-Muslim states as it expands across the globe.

If Muslims are unable to convince their non-Muslim neighbors to "embrace Islam," the next step is to unite and form a cohesive community. The community must prepare and wait for the day to "rise against the government by force at a later date, regardless of whether they are the majority or the minority," the al-Ghurabaa site stated. This incredible proposal is followed, as is often the case, by a Koranic quote for evidence. "Allah says: 'Rule by what Allah has revealed (the Koran and *Sunnah*) and do not follow their vain desires, but be aware of them lest they turn you far away from some of that which Allah has sent down to you."[33]

UK jihadis claim that "the verse is so clear-cut and proves that the *sharia* must be implemented by force even if the people do not want it." Verses from the Koran continued to be cited, including one in which Allah instructs his followers to "fight them until there is no more *fitnah* (insurrection) and worship (obedience, submission etc.) is for none but Allah . . . ' (English Koran al-Baqarah, 2:193)."[34]

The al-Ghurabaa website had little time for patient debate and proselytizing aimed at converting the British to Islam. Jihad is the best way to immunize one's self against the *fitnah* and will ensure resistance to falling under the sway of "man-made" laws, one of the greatest forms of infidelity imaginable. "Islam has always been spread by the sword, and it will continue to do so."[35]

This is how jihadis plan to upload the virtual caliphate in Britain: first by seeking to ensure that British Muslims themselves have fallen in line with their Salafi views, and then by launching a violent coup to seize power if attempts at da'wa (or missionizing) fail. No matter how fantastical an illusion their plan appears to be, jihadis are certain in their mission, as Britain learned on July 7, 2005.

It becomes apparent from the messages above that moderate Muslim communities form the primary and most immediate hurdle to jihadis. No Salafi community plotting a violent overthrow of the government can be created if Muslims are divided, with the bulk refraining from active participation and support of jihad. In that light, the al-Ghurabaa websites turned its attention to an often-quoted verse in the Koran that is usually cited to show that force and Islam do not go together, with a view to flipping this interpretation on its head.

"Unfortunately, nowadays one of the greatest misunderstandings of the divine texts is in reference to the verse, '*Laa ikraaha fid-Deen* - There is no compulsion in religion . . . ' (English Koran 2:256). This verse has been falsely interpreted to mean that we cannot force Islam upon the people. However . . . we can clearly see that this is not the case at all."[36]

In what is a radical departure from the traditional understanding of that verse, the jihadis stated that "no compulsion in religion" means that no individual can be forced to convert to Islam. However, it does not mean that the Islamic system of law and order cannot be forced on a society.

"The Messenger Muhammad said: 'I have been ordered to fight mankind until they say, '*Laa ilaaha illallah wa anna Muhammadar Rasool-Ullah* [There is none worthy of worship except Allah and Muhammad is the Messenger of Allah].' If they say that, their blood and wealth will be saved from me," according to an Islamic hadith used here to back up the jihadi worldview. The message to moderate Muslims is simple: your peace-oriented understanding of Islam is wrong. Islamic sources clearly call for bloody war to be waged in order to ensure that Islam is the dominant political system on earth.[37]

While individuals retain the right not to convert to Islam, society as a collective "must at least live by the laws of Islam; either way, the people have a choice of which religion they want to follow, but they have no choice of whether to live by the *sharia* or not – this is the meaning [of the quote]," the jihadis explained.[38]

One need look no further than Muhammad who invited unbelievers to embrace Islam as a system of governance, the website said. If they refused, then holy war was waged to achieve that goal. This web post relied heavily on hadiths instructing Muslims to make infidels an offer they cannot refuse: accept Islamic rule or die.

What happens if infidels accept Islam as a political regime but cling to their own religions? In such a scenario, the infidels must pay a special tax known as the *jizya*, the website explained. "If they refuse to accept Islam, demand from them the *jizya* [tax]. If they agree to pay, accept it from them and hold off your hands. If they refuse to pay the tax, seek Allah's help and fight them.'"[39]

The jizya is one of the most symbolic forms of the caliphate system's dominance. After paying the jizya, al-Ghurabaa continued, "the non-Muslim will be under a covenant, thus making it prohibited for any Muslim to violate his sanctity."[40] Once the jizya has been paid, the caliphate's soldiers can focus their efforts elsewhere. The superiority and authority of their state has been recognized by all its inhabitants.

9
The Ministry of Morality

The virtual caliphate—a borderless entity—is demonstrating an extraordinary ability to micromanage the lives of its "citizens," mostly because, so far, they have all willingly joined the caliphate movement out of adherence to a cult-like ideology. On a daily basis, representatives of the virtual caliphate dish out instructions on every aspect of life to those seeking guidance online. With no verifiable Islamic credentials, these online preachers insist that their guidelines are entrenched in indisputable Islamic evidence.

"It has been made very clear that we do not forsake Allah for the sake of anybody," a British Islamist leader told listeners on the Paltalk audio chat network in January 2006. Endless prohibitions must be adhered to out of an effort to avoid "forsaking Allah."[1]

In this vein, a talk delivered late at night on Paltalk by this charismatic deputy of Omar Bakri explained to young British Muslim listeners the conditions under which they were permitted to study at universities. "What is not allowed for you is to free mix in order to study those issues, or to disobey Allah in any other issues," the speaker, who identified himself as Abu Mizaan, declared in a live audio broadcast.[2] "Free mix" is a reference to men and women studying together, a strictly forbidden activity in the eyes of these Islamists.

"Don't shave your beard to get into university, don't start to free mix. And don't study any haram [forbidden] subjects. Anything that is going to expose you to kuffar, do not study that issue," Abu Mizaan said.[3] He then listed the subjects followers were permitted to study; medicine, IT were "no problem," he said. But jihadi university students had to tread a careful path in obtaining this knowledge, taking good care not to "disobey Allah" during their studies.

If radicalized students find the balancing act too difficult to manage, they should not hesitate to quit higher education, Abu Mizaan said. Jihad is far more important than university. "Don't let anybody say to you, it's an obligation, it's sinful if you don't go to university. Rather, you are sinful if you don't go to jihad."[4] Such advice will surely fly in the face of the ethics and emphasis on education that many hard-working first-generation Asian immigrants to Britain seek to pass on to their UK-born children.[5]

Abu Mizaan proceeded to answer a series of questions that appeared in text-form on the screen by users in the chat room.

"Next question, what is the ruling on gays?" he said, reading the question off the screen. "Gays, obviously, if they engage in any homosexual act, they will be thrown off the tallest cliff or building or mountain and they will be stoned as well to death."[6]

Islamic law distinguishes between a homosexual who despite living in sin "is still Muslim" and one who "promotes homosexuality," the latter clearly being an infidel, Abu Mizaan said. A homosexual killed for being gay will still be buried with the Muslims, Mizaan explained, but those who go so far as to defend homosexuality have unforgivably strayed from Islam.

Here, in one online chat session, British Muslims have been told how to approach higher education in line with jihadi ideology and have been taught that gays must be killed. The jihadi view on all aspects of life is delivered via the Internet to Muslims who are in the process of radicalization and are eager for answers.

"The Jews and Christians do not believe in Allah and do not believe in the hereafter that we believe," Abu Mizaan told his listeners. Jews and Christians have not accepted Islam, making them infidels, the category of people "we've been ordered to fight." Until the day of judgment arrives, "that is the final word on the jihad."[7]

One of the listeners then posted a question to Mizaan about anger. Is anger allowed, the forum member asked, or is it forbidden as "some Muslims claim?" The prophet Muhammad proscribed an anger-free life, Mizaan replied, encouraging self-control. Anger, once unleashed, can lead a Muslim to transgress his religion and will end up causing the believer to be hostile to those around him. "So don't become angry, except for the sake of Allah." Listeners should forget Mizaan's advice about anger if they encounter criticisms of Islam. Suddenly, anger and even rage are positive traits. "You will become angry only when you see somebody insult Allah or you see someone insult the messenger, you become angry for the sake of Allah."[8]

Abu Mizaan then recounted how an Islamic historical character became so enraged when a "Jew insulted Allah in front of him, he became angry and he punched him immediately in his face. And it is said no one saw anyone punch like that, and it is said he nearly killed him."[9] Anger in defense of Islam is a commandment, Abu Mizaan said.

"So yes, you become angry for the sake of Allah, for the sake of his law, for the sake of any attack on the Muslims, or any attack on the messenger. You have to become angry when you see the rule of Allah being violated."[10]

In his answer to a question on anger, Mizaan told his listeners not to have an angry disposition before ironically giving them the blueprints to being in a permanent state of rage. According to the virtual caliphate's moral approach, a non-Islamist environment must not only be rejected ideologically, but also emotionally; anger, rage, and hatred must constantly be expressed toward non-Muslims and Muslims who do not agree with the jihadi path.

Mizaan then took his lesson in anger one step further by using the question on anger to attack moderate Muslims, saying that those who do not become angry with critics of Islam are as bad as any of Islam's enemies. "So we must get angry, whenever we see haram [forbidden acts], whenever we see kuffr [infidelity], or shirk [transgression of Islamic law]. You don't become angry for the sake of personal issues, and you don't let your anger cause you to transgress and disobey Allah."[11]

The illustration of the follower who is said to have struck a Jewish man for "mocking Muhammad" is held up as an example of model behavior on the part of a good Muslim. This is how the ministry of morality instills an instinct of violent, even murderous, rejection to any criticism of Islam. If internalized by recruits in the West, such values are sure to place them on a direct collision course with the democratic, liberal values of Western society.

The ministry of morality played a key role in orchestrating the reaction of radical Muslims in Britain to the controversy surrounding the Danish newspaper cartoons of Muhammad. Briefly recalled, in September 2005, the Danish newspaper *Jyllands-Posten* held a competition for cartoonists who were asked to submit drawings of Muhammad. The competition was meant to symbolize the newspaper's commitment to free speech. A number of cartoons were submitted, most of which portrayed Islam's prophet as a brutal and threatening leader. The cartoons sparked violent demonstrations around the world. Many of the demonstrations, especially in Western countries, were organized on the Internet.

"If you are not angry over the cartoons you are worse than the cartoon drawers," the title of a crowded Paltalk chat room cried out. On the Saved Sect website, Internet activists were busy preparing their response that would send shockwaves around Britain and the world. The website announced that a demonstration would be held outside the Danish Embassy on February 3, 2006. "We therefore call on Muslims everywhere to demonstrate their anger, to raise their voices in condemnation and to forbid the evil of man-made law and its proponents", the event was billed on the website.[12]

UK Internet jihadis immediately seized on the cartoon as proof that their long-held conspiracy theory was accurate and that the enemies of Islam were indeed closing in. According to Saved Sect, the cartoons posed an immediate "challenge for Muslims to either put up or shut up, to accept insults to the Messengers of Allah (SWT) or to condemn such blasphemy, to abide by the law of the land or call for the Sharee'ah [sharia]."[13]

The cartoons were the latest versions of Crusader propaganda, and anger over the cartoons was the first step to issuing the proper response, the establishment of Islamic law (the caliphate) across Europe. Time is running out, the Saved Sect warned, as the European conspirators were encircling the Muslims. "European countries have gathered together side by side, shoulder to shoulder, confronting the common enemy, a day after the State of the Union address by George Bush where he said that so-called radical Islam needed to be defeated." The signs were everywhere, visitors to the website learned. One only needed to connect the dots to see where incidents similar to the one involving the Danish cartoons were leading. First Islamic dress was banned in France, then jihadi leaders were arrested Britain, and "Muslims are now required to remain silent when the Messenger Muhammad (SAW)'s honor is attacked."[14] Drastic action was needed.

But this latest assault can be turned on its head. "This latest episode in the war against Islam and Muslims is probably the issue which will unite all Muslims in condemnation," the Saved Sect said triumphantly, predicting that Muslims would rally around the honor of their prophet.[15]

Jihadis plotted a march route in which operatives would gather at the Danish embassy and march to the Norwegian, French, German, Italian, and Spanish embassies, "Insha' Allah. The cartoons that appeared in the newspapers and which insult the Messenger Muhammad (SAW) carry the death penalty in Islam for the perpetrators, since the Prophet said, '**Whoever insults a Prophet kill him**.'"[16] (emphasis in original).

On July 19, 2007, four men were sentenced to prison terms in Britain for their roles in the demonstrations. Twenty-four-year-old Mizanur Rahman (who could well be the "Abu Mizaan" who delivered "morality" sermons on Paltalk; in an October 2005 webcast, Mizaan, referring to his web name, told listeners, "That is my real name"); twenty-seven-year-old Umran Javed; and twenty-five-year-old Abdul Muhid were convicted of incitement to murder and sentenced to six years behind bars. Thirty-two-year-old Abdul Saleem was sentenced to four years for incitement to racial hatred.

Much of the men's planning of the demonstration, as already seen, took place on the Internet. From their perspective, the demonstration was a stunning success. On February 3, 2006, nearly five hundred people gathered outside the Danish embassy in London. They held placards that read: "Europe you will pay, your 9/11 is on the way," "7/7 is on its way," "Freedom go to hell," and "Europe you'll come crawling, when the Mujahideen come roaring."[17] Shouts of "jihad, jihad" and calls for Britain to be bombed were screamed through megaphones.

One demonstrator, Omar Khayam, wore a mock suicide-bomb vest to the demonstration. The terrifying display received international press coverage, though little attention was given to the scene of where the protest was organized and incited—the web space occupied by Britain's al Qaeda affiliated activists. "Muslims take their ideology and belief very seriously and any insult to any Messengers and Prophets will never be tolerated," the Saved Sect professed on its website, thriftily using the incident to dish out jihadi morality.[18] Muslims must love Muhammad more than their parents and even themselves, the website said.

Had a caliphate been in existence at this time, transgressors who dared insult Muhammad would face the proscribed sentence for such a crime: death. "However, sadly we find that we live in an era where there is not one country in the world implementing the Shareeah [sharia]." The Saved Sect used the cartoons to turn the wrath of followers on Muslim states that are not ruled by Islamic law. These fifty-five states are far worse than the Muhammad cartoonists, the jihadis said, because their ignorance of Islam "ensures that Muslims are kept in subservience to the West."[19]

The same Muslim states that "do not lift a finger" to help out Muslims in places such as Iraq, Palestine, Chechnya and Afghanistan offered only lip service in response to the Muhammad cartoons, the website charged, due to their fear of being "overthrown by an angry Muslim population."[20]

Without this fear, "not a word would have been mentioned about the current incident from the leaders of Saudi Arabia, Egypt, Bahrain, Pakistan, Kuwait etc.," the website added. Further, these events have all been prophesized by Muhammad and mark the beginning of a final showdown between the believers and unbelievers. "We, the Followers of Ahl us-Sunnah wal Jamma, call upon all mosques to rally their congregations this Friday (after prayers) to come to this significant demonstration. . . . O Muslims, let this incident be the start of redoubling our efforts to establish the Shareeah [sharia] on earth so that the Khaleefah [caliphate] can once again be the shield behind which the Muslims defend themselves and from behind which we can eradicate man-made law."[21]

The Ministry of Morality on Women

As noted, the protest organized online materialized into reality and attracted international notoriety for its direct and uncensored calls for terrorist attacks in Europe and Britain. When the protest's ringleaders were sentenced to jail, female British radicalized Muslims, covered head to toe in veils, held their own demonstration. The *Daily Mail* reported, "Outside the court, around 40 demonstrators—most hiding their faces—chanted and held placards. Among them were a gaggle of women in burkas, who held up a sign which read: 'British police go to hell.'"[22]

Attitudes toward women help define the society and culture of any political movement. The culture of radical jihadi doctrines can be gauged by views expressed on women. So what does the ministry of morality say about the role of Muslim women?

The Al-Ghurabaa website released a document called "Women and Jihad," which set out to clarify the role of women in jihad. A woman can ensure her place in paradise if she looks after the affairs of her home and husband while he is out fighting, the website explained. But women can also take a far more active role in the fighting.

"However it is also well documented that Rasool-Allaah [Muhammad] always took one of his wives with him to the battlefield," the website continued.[23] A hadith of Aisha, one of Muhammad's wives, follows: "Whenever the Prophet intended to proceed on a journey, he used to draw lots amongst his wives and would take the one upon whom the lot fell. Once, before setting out for jihad, he drew lots amongst us and the lot came to me; so I went with the Prophet." If Aisha came with Muhammad to jihad when Islam was first founded in the seventh century, married Muslim women in the twenty-first century can do the same.

The document went on to outline women's supportive roles on the battlefield, including "encouraging the mujahideen to stand firm."[24] This behavior was exemplified by the wife and sister of Omar Sharif, a British suicide bomber who, along with an accomplice, murdered three Israeli citizens in a suicide bomb attack on a Tel Aviv pub in 2003.

Sharif's wife, Tahira Tabassum, later went on trial for failing to reveal details of the attack, while Sharif's sister, Parveen, was accused of encouraging her brother to go through with the bombing. "'We did not spend a long time together in this world but I hope through Allah's mercy and your patience we can spend eternity together,'" Omar Sharif wrote in an e-mail to Tahira shortly before embarking on the suicide bombing. "'Plan now and get rid of any material you may consider problematic,'" he advised.[25]

Parveen told her brother via e-mail that "'we all have to be firm and focused . . . there is really no time to be weak and emotional.'"[26] Astonishingly, Parveen and Tahira were acquitted of all charges. There is also strong evidence to suggest that Tahira Tabassum was linked to Omar Bakri. As the *London Times* reported, Tahira "had written the mobile phone number of Omar Bakri Muhammad at the end of notes that she made on a lecture about suicide bombings."[27]

In October 2005, on the Paltalk jihadi chat room, user Veiled Flower eerily asked what a fiancée of a holy warrior should do if he were preparing to martyr himself. She was instructed by the online speaker, Mizaan, to encourage him as much as possible in order to assure herself "a place in paradise."[28]

Perhaps the most chilling message delivered to radicalized women was given by Sheikh Omar Bakri himself, who answered a female listener asking whether she needed permission from her husband to become a suicide bomber in January 2005.

A female listener with the username Mujaidah asked Bakri whether "sisters are allowed to do suicide bombings if the intentions are correct?" Bakri replied, "It happened many times in Palestine, in Chechnya, in Russia . . . this is no problem, there is no restriction."[29]

Islamic Awakening features a "special selection for special sisters" on its website, containing "true stories of some heroic contemporary women whose husbands are either engaged in fighting or have attained the ultimate success of martyrdom."[30]

Indeed, al Qaeda appears to have taken granting women permission to become suicide bombers one step further and has begun actively using the virtual caliphate to recruit female jihadis, as Pakistan's *Daily Times* reported in 2005. "Islamic extremists are looking to recruit women and are trying to do so mainly through the Internet, according to an Italian intelligence report."[31]

"The recruits, the report adds, 'are now also being sought among the female audience,' and an Internet journal has been created especially with the purpose of attracting female warriors," the article continued.

The jihad battlefield is, however, the only arena in which jihadis grant women equal rights. In all other areas, online jihadi literature and forums place women in a subservient cage.

As the South African Islamic Internet site TheMajlis.net explains, "Happiness in a marriage is the product of . . . total obedience to the husband. Without display of good conduct, happiness in marriage is not possible."[32]

After being married, the young wife should abandon her family and regard only her husband's family as her own family, TheMajlis.net counsels. "His parents are now her parents. Her parents have become strangers to her," the online guide states to newly married Muslim women.[33]

In any event of conflict between the wife's family and her husband, the woman must unquestionably take her husband's side, no matter the wrongs and rights of the dispute. Under no circumstances must the wife stand up for her family. Instead, "she should understand that she has to pass her life with her husband, not with her parents or her brothers. Even if her husband unjustly speaks ill of her parents and brothers, she should not display annoyance. She should not pull up her face nor make any comment which will inflame him. She should employ her intelligence, *be it defective*, and convey to her husband that she is on his side, not on the side of her family, because now her only family is her husband's family,"[34] (italics added for emphasis).

Women should not concern themselves with standing up for themselves or dealing with wrongs, as "Allah Ta'ala will take her husband to task for his injustices. It is not her concern. *Her concern is to serve her husband, keep him happy and please him* in all lawful things,"[35] (italics added for emphasis).

These are the instructions of Allah and Muhammad, who command a Muslim wife to fully submit to her husband. "Her happiness (her Jannat) is inextricably interwoven with his pleasure."[36]

Women by nature are far more likely to displease their creator than men, the website adds. They are especially guilty of "ingratitude to their husbands," a quality that led Muhammad to say that "most inmates of Jahannum [hell] will be women. Wives should heed this warning . . . and struggle against . . . this vile emotional urge."[37]

TheMajlis.net lays out expectations of women off the battlefield held by all Islamist movements—they are to use their "defective" intellect to appease and serve their master-husbands.

10
The Ministry of Finance

In preparation for the establishment of an Islamic state, the virtual caliphate's ministry of finance plans its future financial policies. The most pressing related issue is terrorist financing. The Internet is filled with al Qaeda activists and leaders exhorting followers to donate to the jihad.

Financial jihad—raising money for the holy warriors—is seen as a natural second-best alternative by jihadis to physical fighting and forms a major part of jihadi activities in Western capitals. Donating to the jihad is often seen as being equally important to physically carrying it out.

An electronic guide to the financial jihad, currently circulating jihadi websites, touts the Koran as the original source for the call to give generously for holy war. Authored by Mufti Khubiab Sahib, the guide, titled *Essential Provision of the Mujahid*, argues that the virtues of providing financial support "abounds in the Holy Koran and the Revered Sunnah. And the virtues of spending in the jihad . . . and the admonition for those who do not participate in such a virtuous deed, also abound in the Holy Koran and the Revered Sunnah."[1]

Money is no less important than power to carry out jihad, Sahib writes, adding that jihadi organizations should establish a joint and centralized "financial department."[2] The blueprints for a ministry of finance emerge on the Internet.

In the past, when a caliphate existed, "the jihad was on the lips of every Muslim," Sahib laments. Holy warriors then were the most esteemed members of society, and "to provide financial assistance for the jihad was considered as an act of devotion, but now the situation has changed considerably."[3]

The fall of the caliphate has placed the burden of financial donations on the shoulders of a few wealthy Muslims. Despite these Muslims' best intentions, their donations could never come near to the needed funds for jihad.

Sahib points to the mounting costs needed to operate jihadi forces around the world, facing massive hi-tech, well-financed Western military forces. "The back breaking expenses of the jihad are on the increase day by day, because due to the indifference of Muslims, the enemy have amassed a formidable military force. To confront these massive and powerful military forces is a monumental task and requires huge resources."[4]

Without cash to fight the jihad, Muslims will face a defeat that will set them back for centuries, he warns. The answer, Sahib proposes, is the establishment of a ministry of finance.

Sahib praises the tireless war currently being waged by jihadis who are hopelessly outnumbered by an infinitely more powerful enemy. He optimistically observes that despite their shortfalls in resources, "the *mujahideen* are gaining the upper hand day by day. But still the acute need for resources could not be ignored."[5]

This is where the need for a solid financial base comes in, as it will guarantee a victory for the jihad and form the underpinnings of the caliphate that will soon be declared. Sahib lists three basic principles that are to guide his ministry of finance: dignity, to ensure that only honest men handle the funds; protection, to ensure that the funds are processed through a set channel protected by accountability and checks; and piety, to stave off the qualities of greed and vanity, qualities that can deplete the funds before they reach their intended destinations.

Similarly, jihad fundraising is a serious affair that must be pursued in an appropriate way. Undignified fundraising tactics will harm the reputation of the holy fighters and end up turning donors off, Sahib notes.

Sahib trumpets savings and investments as a sound means to store funds, stressing the importance of not squandering the jihad's entire treasure chest in a short span of time. "Therefore an attempt ought to be made to invest the available finances in some sound and profitable ventures and businesses with a minimum risk of losses."[6]

His advice for jihadis to invest funds raised for the jihad in profitable businesses is a call for the creation of front companies that can launder jihad money and provide additional funds through profits. Jihadis pursue such activities on a daily basis, and counterterrorism agencies are constantly attempting to untangle the long web of interlinked Islamist businesses aimed at raising money for terrorists. Many of these fronts take the shape of charities.

"If a policy of putting aside a small part of the available funds, as future capital savings, is pursued then with Allah's help, the Movements would become self-sufficient in financing any future organisational and other expenditures and the steady flow of the income will become a spring board for expanding the activities of the jihad," Sahib declares.[7]

One example is the Islamic American Relief Agency, a charity created by the Islamic African Relief Agency (IARA). In October 2004, the U.S. Treasury found that IARA had transferred millions of dollars to terrorist networks run by Osama Bin Laden and has since frozen IARA's assets. IARA's chief, Mubarak Hamed, is personally accused of raising $5 million for al Qaeda during a fund-raising trip to Sudan and other locations in the Middle East in 2000. The pretense of being a charity allowed the IARA to raise funds for the jihad in a secure manner, in line with Sahib's guidelines.

A good fund-raising drive is to be accompanied by a "department of propagation and information," aimed at educating Muslims on the virtues of being generous for jihad, Sahib says. There can be no understating the holiness of the act. Prospective donors must be told in a booklet that "the contribution in the jihad entails the greatest reward from Allah."[8]

Another booklet should be distributed that awakens Muslims to the infidels' nefarious intentions toward the Muslims. "In addition to this, these booklets should also contain the facts and figures of the Mujahideen's expenses in detail."[9]

Sahib cannot repeat often enough his claim that the act of donating to the jihad is deeply rooted in Islamic law. He says holy warriors must themselves explain to the rest of the Muslims that the onus is on the masses to financially support the war. "According to the Revered Sharia of Islam, the mujahideen are obliged to propagate the virtues of spending in the jihad, as pronounced in the Holy Koran and the Revered *Sunnah*."[10] The fund-raising should not go on indefinitely, however. After the case has been made to the Muslims, it is their decision whether to donate money. Those who choose not to reach into their pockets should not be asked again, as this would be a humiliation to the holiest of causes. "If some Muslims do not wish to participate in spending for the jihad, then to knock on their door would be an insult to the *mujahideen*, as they are appealing for financial help only for the victory of Islam."[11]

In his uploaded writings, Sahib also lays out detailed plans on how his proposed ministry will take shape. The ministry must act as a central organ in preparation for the caliphate's establishment. It must compile a complete inventory of its possessions and properties, no matter how small and seemingly minor. This inventory should include the weapons held by the jihadi army.

In Sahib's vision, the ministry of finance will become the dominant organization within the emerging caliphate, claiming responsibility for the assets of the caliphate's various emerging ministries.

"Even the establishment of a new office in a foreign country will be accountable to and administered by the Finance Department for its resources, properties, materials and finances. In the event of the closure of a regional office, the Finance Department will also be responsible for collecting all the belongings of that office and entering into the records and checking against the acquisitions."[12]

Such an approach will ensure that one body will enjoy "centralized control over the whole organization," Sahib writes.[13]

Sahib tries not to get carried away by visions of a triumphant caliphate and therefore brings his followers back to the current reality, where those who plot and carry out war for the caliphate's birth are wanted individuals. This reality means that a range of precautions must be taken when dealing with the jihad's assets.

Assets of any sort owned by jihadis should never be registered in the name of jihad organizations or leaders because of the twin threats of a sudden ban on the organization and/or assassination or arrest of the leader by the enemy's agents. In any of these scenarios, exposed resources could be lost. Subterfuge is essential so long as the caliphate is still a dream.

Money Transfers

We have seen how the virtual caliphate's ministry of finance encourages Muslims to donate generously to the jihad and how the Internet is used to discuss blueprints for a centralized ministry of finance.

But where do the physical money transfers to terrorists take place? Aaron Weisburd, author of Internet Haganah, a website that systemically tracks and helps shut down jihadi sites, wrote the following via e-mail to the author. "What jihadis do to raise money is commit crime. In the real world they are involved in things such as document forgery, organized retail theft and drug dealing (e.g. Hezbollah and hashish, al-Qaeda and heroin). In the virtual world the crime of choice is credit card fraud/identity theft."[14]

Weisburd is a founding member of the Society for Internet Research (SOFIR) and has amassed a wealth of knowledge on the gray zones linking online jihadi activities and real-world terrorist activities.

"In the investigation that the Society for Internet Research conducted regarding the activities of [an online jihadi with the username] Younis Tsouli Irhabi007 and his associates, we identified multiple occurrences where stolen identities and credit card accounts were used to register domain names and pay the bills for a number of al-Qaeda websites," Weisburd wrote.[15]

"Tsouli and his companions, including the Palestinian Tariq al-Dour, spent only a small portion of the money they stole on internet-related expenses. Most of it was spent buying supplies for the *mujahideen*. They laundered money by running it through an assortment of online gambling sites and through various eGold and CashU type services. They raised £1.2 million in just a year or two," Weisburg communicated, providing a valuable glimpse at how jihadi agents use the Internet for jihad financing.[16]

"A few years ago we were investigating www.jihad-algeria.com, a site which at the time was the official site of the Algerian al-Qaeda franchise [GSPS, now called al-Qaeda of the Maghreb]. There were 13 sites sharing a single IP address and all operated by the same two individuals. One site was Jihad-algeria.com. The others were all related to various online scams—fake bank sites, fake shipping company sites, phishing sites, etc. Included in the sites was an excellent copy of the site of Chase Manhattan Bank. In fact, the only 'genuine' site on the server was the terrorist site."[17]

Weisburd said that the case of the online jihadi with the username Irhabi007 provides a rare insight into the problem because the suspect was arrested and openly tried, allowing several details on his activities to be revealed. Irabi007's case is unusual, as captures of jihadi operatives taking place in repressive Middle Eastern countries hardly ever hit the headlines and the fate of those captured remains unknown. "Often we will observe signs of criminal activity related to online jihadi activity, but we don't get feedback regarding the findings of the criminal investigations conducted based on our reports. In the case of the Algerian site, for instance, all I know for sure is that the main webmaster was captured in a cyber cafe in Damascus and turned over to the Algerians by Syria. I doubt we will ever hear from him again."[18]

Making Poverty History

Only the caliphate can make poverty history, Khilafah.com proclaims to its readers. According to jihadi financial planners spreading their message online, it is only the proposed caliphate that has the God-given answers needed to totally eliminate the scourge of poverty, itself a product of defective man-made rules guiding the allocation of resources and economies.

"Islam views poverty through a different lens relative to that being presented by the developed world and at the same time has a number of rules which would eradicate poverty," Khilafah.com promises Muslims.[19]

Defining poverty as the lack of three basic resources needed for a healthy life—food, clothing, and shelter—the website attacks the West's ever-changing definition of poverty as being relative.

What, then, is the ministry of finance's solution for making poverty history? Any resource regarded as vital for the general public should be nationalized under the caliphate state and be considered public property. Khilafah.com falls back on a hadith and quotes Muhammad as saying: "Muslims are partners in three things: in water, pastures and fire." That short list is then turned by the caliphate's financial planners into a range of utilities requiring nationalization. Using analogies, the authors manage to cover much ground based on water, pastures, and fire. "Water sources, forests of firewood, oil fields, electricity plants, motorways, rivers, seas, lakes, public canals, gulfs, straits, dams etc. cannot be owned by individuals," Khilafah.com rules.[20]

Assets that are not vital for the general public can, conversely, be owned privately. The caliphate's virtual architects boast that public utilities will not be at the mercy of monopolies because of this policy. Further, charity, a pillar of Islam, would replace taxes.

The socialist-like blueprint for overall state control of public utilities combined with some private ownership appears to most resemble the Chinese system. What is beyond doubt, however, is that the ministry of finance has a plan on how the caliphate should handle its economy. Many ideas are employed to reward hard work, such as the granting of ownership of derelict land to any farmer who came to cultivate it. "Whoever cultivated a land that is not owned by anybody, then he deserves it more," a hadith quoting Muhammad reads.

In the Arab world, the authors of Khilafah.com claim that there is "an abundance of water and a very fertile land . . . this land has been left unused due to people residing in the main towns."[21] One rule of Islam could provide all of the solutions to this problem.

Those in the cities who cannot support themselves or their families financially should not go on the dole, but should instead be moved to the countryside and given the tools to become farmers.

"Hence, much of this agricultural land will be given to people who cannot support themselves so that they can help provide the state's agricultural needs."[22]

Agricultural Policy

A reestablished caliphate is meant to reign over all lands in which modern-day Muslim states exist, and the caliphate will therefore be in the position to bring skills common in one part of the world to another where such knowledge is scarce. "Turkish farmers are some of the most skilled in the world whilst Pakistani farmers are some of the most technologically advanced," Khilafah.com says.[23] These are the people who need to teach their fellow Muslims how to farm. The caliphate state should protect its farmers from a tumultuous market and an unpredictable climate.

After the caliphate is born, agriculture will be one of the most important and urgent areas for the new state, which is why large amounts of funds must be invested in agricultural policy, Khilafah.com urges. "Only the development of the defence industry and the sustenance of oil and gas industry should be higher on the agenda."[24]

"Agriculture will also become, inshallah one of the biggest sources of employment hence creating jobs and circulating more wealth around the economy," Khilfah.com explains.[25] Thus, the new Islamic state must invest heavily in the latest agricultural machinery and technology.

The authors of Khilafah.com take a surprising regime as their role model in this field:

> It is noteworthy to mention that North Korea has had a sound agricultural policy in the past that it developed after WW2 in three stages along communist lines. However, North Korea finds that when it wishes to export its machinery the US and European markets are closed to them due to protectionist measures. The Khilafah [caliphate] should create favourable trade terms such that we are able to purchase North Koran [*sic*] agricultural machinery whilst benefiting from their agricultural techniques.[26]

The agricultural-policy authors of Khilafah.com appear to ignore the reports of mass famines and starvations that have ravaged North Korea, as they plot a future trading relationship with pariah entities known for their disastrous management of agriculture and the economy.

Capitalism: The Enemy

According to Khilafah.com, the poverty seen today in the Muslim world is the fault of only one force: capitalism. The website points a finger at "a whole host of capitalist ideas which severely restrict the distribution of wealth. The khilafah [caliphate] will immediately up-root all reminisce of the capitalist system and apply Islam in its entirety. If one was to examine the effects of such rules it is very clear poverty would disappear."[27] Taxes would be banished by the ministry of finances, as "Islam does not have a concept of income tax, nor value added tax, nor excise duties, nor national insurance contributions and so forth."[28]

Wealth—not income—would be taxed, which, Khilafah.com argues, would result in great savings for the average earner. Interest rates should be abolished, as they create extortionist mortgage traps spanning three decades. Payments for cars and other material things leave next to nothing of people's earnings. Worse yet, because of interest rates, people are prone to leaving capital in a bank to accumulate interest, which is an impediment to the circulation of wealth. The caliphate would introduce a host of rules to ensure that the circulation of money continues to flow, and the only ones who would face taxation would be those who "hoard their wealth."[29]

"In Islam incentives not to spend are non existent, interest is forbidden and hoarding is taxed. Having no interest means there is no incentive to leave money in a bank account as it will not accumulate interest, but instead be taxed if it's held for a year."[30] In the caliphate, high-interest savings accounts for the rich would be a thing of the past.

Similarly, land not used for three years can be confiscated by the state, thereby ending family monopolies in the third world. These families are described as inheriting large swaths of properties from departing imperial powers.

The caliphate's financial policymakers look with horror upon the subprime lending crisis and the credit financial crisis of 2008, pointing to the events as further proof that there are inherent flaws of modern man-made capitalism. There would be no stock market in the caliphate.

"Paper such as shares, bonds and debt as a form of commodity are non existent in Islam, the only types of investment are in real goods which ensures the economy continually generates wealth."[31]

Khilfah.com claims that with this general blueprint, all Muslims can be yanked free of poverty. The caliphate's divine financial management policies could then be exhibited to Latin American and African states that have been enslaved to American and World Bank regulations, the authors add.

"The Muslim world has been blessed with fertile land, water and minerals which if dealt with correctly can easily solve the poverty in the Muslim world. What must also be clear that the mere production of agricultural goods is not the solution to poverty its distribution is where the problem lies and Turkey is a good example of this, 20 percent of its 70 million population live in poverty even though it is a world leader in agricultural production," Khilafah notes.[32]

Banishing interest rates and taxing large savings in order to force money to circulate the economy is certainly counterintuitive to Western economic instincts.

Unsurprisingly, individual capital ventures and financial independence are seen as Western evils, and in between capitalism and socialism, the ministry of finance certainly veers toward the latter, though it also has its own unique formulas that by no means can be seen as socialist. The ideas proposed do not appear to be designed with any of the issues that affect twenty-first-century economies in mind, such as foreign investment, technological innovation, and the information revolution. Nevertheless, a wholly alternative financial blueprint has been set out online. The virtual caliphate's ministry of finance—a mere idea in cyberspace at this stage—would like to implement these policies.

11
Electronic Warfare

The virtual caliphate's members have repeatedly been encouraged by fellow online activists to "take over" non-Islamist websites and engage in arguments to spread their ideology.

Another more damaging form of this same effort is the ongoing attempt by Islamist web users to electronically attack (or hack) "enemy sites" and render them unusable. Just as the physical world is divided by Islamists into the land of war and the House of Islam, the Internet, too, is split along the same lines, and members of the virtual caliphate see it as their duty to attack or convert non-Islamist areas of the Internet. Certainly, such attacks could be directed at official websites of targeted countries, some of which could be vital for communications or other functions.

In 2003 a statement appeared on the now-nonexistent al Qaeda website, al-Farouq, signed by an unknown man called Muhammad Bin Ahmed Al-Salem. Al-Salem, possibly a pseudonym, authored an e-book titled *The 39 Principles of Jihad*, in which he declared, "Al-Salem attributes paramount importance to the Internet as a component for Jihad. He calls believers to join the Jihad by participating in Internet forums to defend Islam and the Mujahideen, to preach Jihad and to encourage Muslims to learn about this sacred duty. . . . Computer experts are asked to use their skills and experience in destroying American, Jewish and secular websites as well as morally corrupt web sites."[1]

In July 2007, the Information Week website reported on a new and worrying development for global cyberspace.[2] The article examined a new application, called

Electronic Jihad, that offers jihadis a way to launch an attack on websites "perceived to be anti-Islamic."[3]

Jihadi websites, such as al-jinan.org, seized on the program as a welcome new weapon. The application is one in a series of attempts to make accessible the option of launching Internet attacks on desired targets. The attacks typically target the IP addresses of unwanted websites and knock the servers hosting the website off the Internet.

"The Electronic Jihad application comes with a user-friendly Microsoft Windows-like interface that allows users to choose from a list of target websites. The list is provided courtesy of al-jinan.org. After a target is selected, a jihadi can select an attack speed—weak, medium, or strong—before hitting the 'attack button,'" Information Week reported.

Abdul Hameed Bakier, a counterterrorism intelligence analyst, takes Electronic Jihad seriously. Information Week cited an article written in June 2008 by Bakier for Terrorism Focus, published by the Jamestown Foundation, in which he described the application as the start of a new era in electronic jihadi attacks: "In the past, different jihadi groups practiced cyberattacks on anti-Islamic websites, but they were never able to sustain a long, organized campaign."[4] With Electronic Jihad, all that may have changed.

Most forms of jihadi online attacks are based on a denial-of-service (DOS) attack, which often takes the form of flooding an Internet site with visits or hits, leaving the server unable to respond to legitimate visitors.

One of the best examples of concentrated online attacks from across the Muslim world came as a response to the cartoons of the prophet Muhammad, published by Danish newspaper *Jyllands-Posten*. The cartoons, which sparked a storm of rioting around the globe, also saw thousands of virtual attacks on Danish websites deemed to have supported the cartoons' publication.

Security Pro News reported during the height of the virtual attack that "Muslum [*sic*] hackers continue their retaliatory assault on Danish websites over the political cartoons run in Danish newspapers last year and more recently in other European publications. As this story is being written, the number is up to 1819 Danish site[s] alone and continues to rise."[5]

Muslim hackers also targeted the personal blog of American political commentator Michelle Malkin, who featured the cartoons on her website, after she made an appearance on the FOX News Network to discuss the drawings.[6]

"Last Tuesday, during or immediately after my appearance on Fox News Channel to discuss the Mohammed Cartoons, this blog was hit by a large, foreign-based denial-of-service attack. Last night, my hosting service notified me that it is receiving ongoing threats from individuals vowing to take down this site—and others along with it—which will presumably continue until I take down the cartoons," Malkin wrote on her blog.[7] She posted a few examples of the death threats she received:

> From: monalisa monalisa
> To: writemalkin@gmail.com
> Mailed-By: hotmail.com
> Date: Feb 4, 2006 5:55 PM
> Subject: you are filth
>
> the dishonourable the mean the prostitute I'am a müslim and
> turkish I kill
> you devil you are goto the hell shit the whore
>
> ———
>
> From: greatmastafa
> Mailed-By: web.de
> To: writemalkin@gmail.com
> Date: Feb 11, 2006 9:41 PM
> Subject: mohammed
>
> you have one day to delete all pictures of mohammed from your server, or
> i hack this site and delete all files on this server. ok
> mohammed have never a face. dou you now.
> for ever islam.[8]

The Jamestown Foundation reported that the wave of online attacks in response to the Muhammad cartoon exhibited the competence and sophistication of "the internet mujahideen."[9] The al-Ghurabaa site coordinated a twenty-four-hour-long assault on Danish newspapers, a hacking effort that became a cause célèbre. Forum members excitedly discussed how to enlarge their efforts.

Hacking for Allah

In addition to denial-of-service attacks, hostile online jihadis can also employ the weapon of hacking a website, in which they seize control of a site and provide an alternative webpage to greet its visitors. The hacked site usually carries a provocative message and a signature by the hacker (or hacking group) behind the attack. Jihadi websites have not only encouraged followers to hack enemy websites, they have also begun providing tips and tools for would-be hackers to accomplish their objectives.

A member of the al-Firdaws jihadi forum began a guide to hacking with a prayer. The guide can be downloaded along with diagrams explaining how to insert the word "explosion" in large, red graphic letters, complete with visual effects on a targeted website. Detailed instructions and the HTML code needed to achieve the desired effect are also given.

The online guide shows how to manipulate text and improve its visual clarity. Once a website has been penetrated, hackers will replace its original content with their own message. In the case of using the word "explosion," the aim is to allow jihadi hackers to threaten bomb attacks, manipulating Western websites in order to deliver their warnings.

Just as virtual jihadis proudly post videos of "martyrdom operations" on the Internet, a new trend has emerged in which jihadis exhibit successful hacks of other websites. One such video documents an attack on the *Jyllands-Posten* newspaper. The video begins by comparing Danes to pigs, showing a manipulated image of a Danish man with a pig's ears and nose.

The video has an Islamic song in the background. It shows the body of Dutch filmmaker Theo van Gough lying in the street, with a knife protruding from his chest. In November 2004, Van Gough had been murdered by a Muslim youth who took offense to his film on Islam.

The online video is essentially a threat to those in Europe who are perceived to insult Islam. You are in grave danger, flashing red text indicates, against the background of a skull. The video then threatens mass hackings against offending websites.

The video goes into split-screen mode, showing a screen shot of a computer being used to hack a website. This is what will happen to websites that support the assault on Islam, the video's makers appear to be saying.

The video displays a Windows Explorer window opened to the address of the *Jyllands-Posten* website. "Network error (tcp error)," the message reads. "A communication error occurred . . . for assistance, contact your network support team."[10]

The video had apparently been nothing less than a "documentary" showing the step-by-step process of crashing the *Jyllands-Posten*'s website. Juxtaposing the picture of Van Gough's body next to a hacked website gives a unique insight into the jihadi mentality and message. Anyone or anything that offends jihadis will be destroyed.

Not only can the Internet be used to target websites, but vital national infrastructures such as power grids can also become targets. In an interview with the author, prominent American terrorism expert and executive director of the Investigative Project on Terrorism, Steve Emerson, expressed that U.S. national security faces the threat of "terrorist exploitation of open sources to find our vulnerabilities." Emerson listed some of these terrorist objectives: "Downloading open source grids of power installations, US Embassy architectural diagrams, military base configurations, hacking into sensitive sites; and conveyance of surveillance information and photos."[11] This threat is discussed further in chapter 15.

Defensive Techniques Against Cyberattacks

In one of the first conferences of its kind, Israel's Ben-Gurion University of the Negev called together dozens of experts from around the world to discuss security on the Internet in the face of jihadi hackers. The conference was held in June 2007.

Addressing the conference, Yuval Elovici, director of Deutsche Telekom Laboratories at Ben-Gurion University, spelled out the techniques he had been working on to combat the threat and outlined how jihadis were using unwitting individual Internet users to attack vital computer systems in states they viewed as the enemy.

"Everyone is currently connected to [the] Internet, including government agencies. Everyday vulnerabilities are discovered and exploited by hackers to create killer worms," Elovici said.[12] A killer worm is a program that can exploit computer security vulnerabilities and attack vital infrastructure. The most common way to deliver a killer worm is through an application known as a Trojan horse. The Trojan horse can be downloaded onto a computer without the user's knowledge and then can take control of that computer, giving it a set of instructions. Much like a cell in the human body that is being taken over, the computer is hijacked by a foreign entity and used to help the attack along. Computers that come under the control of Trojan horses are known as zombies.

With only 50 percent of websites protected from Trojan horses and other threats, Elovici said, the Western Internet landscape is certainly vulnerable to attack by jihadis.

"Terrorists may create killer worms to attack critical infrastructure. They [jihadis] follow announcements on new operating system vulnerabilities, create a killer worm (based on the vulnerabilities), and launch it through Trojan horses installed by innocent users to avoid being detected. The attack is carried out through home users," Elovici explained. It is "very important to develop technology to prevent users from being infected with Trojan horses," he stressed.[13]

Elovici defined two forms of response to this threat, one defensive and the other offensive. Defensively, firewalls and antiviruses are there to prevent our computers from becoming infected. Offensively, the answer lies in "improving technology for detecting terrorist activities on the web and tracing back the origins of the attack."[14]

Detecting hidden terrorist online activities is a key ability needed for any offensive response, Elovici said. But this is easier said than done, with devices that can mask a web user's IP addresses and networks that have multiple IP addresses, which provide camouflage for online holy warriors.

"One terrorist, say at university, goes to many terror-related pages, it is difficult to differentiate between the terrorist computer and other innocent users," Elovici argued.[15]

One solution lay in separating out the various threads of Internet traffic coming from the multi-user network and "using several analyzers, locate traffic heading back into the network which will include packets from the specific user hidden behind the network. We can see if the content includes access to terror-related websites," Elovici proposed.[16]

Outlining another innovative approach, Elovici told the conference how to prevent jihadis from using innocent third-party Internet users as a vehicle to strike at targets. "We have authored a program to clean traffic through the network service provider," he said. "Currently, traffic is not purified. In the water system, all of the water supply is drinkable. On [the] other hand, traffic from the network service provider is not purified. We suggest cleansing the traffic from within network, thereby protecting customers, and preventing terrorists who might use innocent users to launch attack against critical infrastructure."[17]

Instead of relying on antiviruses to protect individual computers, the Internet service provider can ensure that the Internet traffic reaching its customers has been screened and purified.

"Network service providers have the ability to detect new threats much faster," Elovici said, adding that a "very sophisticated algorithm" was being developed to purify all traffic that arrives at a user's home computer.[18]

Elovici's concept could form one of the leading answers to what may be viewed as the virtual caliphate's electronic attack division. The option of launching Trojan horses in order to insert killer worms into targeted websites could be far less accessible with preventative measures available. In the future, websites such as *Jyllands-Posten*'s may be more immune to the kind of assault it faced in 2005.

12

Online Clashes with Shiites and Iran

With the rise of Iran as a regional power, the high-profile war in Lebanon fought by Shiite Hizbullah against Israel in 2006, and the pivotal role being played by Shiite politicians and militias in Iraq, the Islamic world has experienced increased Sunni-Shiite tensions on a number of levels. Sunnis make up the overwhelming majority of Muslims. Despite Sunnis' numerical advantage, a number of press reports and government statements in Sunni countries, such as Egypt, responded to the recent rise in profile of Shiite- and Iranian-sponsored political and religious organizations. They expressed increasing discomfort with Iran's power and the perceived growing Shiite confidence to take the reins of the Arab-Muslim world.

In Egypt, a number of press reports argued that Shiites were attempting to establish a foothold and convert Sunnis to Shiite Islam, a claim repeated in the widely read pan-Arab daily *Asharq Alawsat*, which is published in London. Sheikh Yusuf al-Qaradawi, a highly influential Muslim Brotherhood–affiliated cleric, issued a warning in September 2008 about an attempt by Shiites to convert Sunnis and expand their sphere of influence in Sunni nations.[1]

The following month, the International Union of Muslim Scholars, a leading forum of clerics, met in Qatar and released a statement backing Qaradawi's warning. The statement called on Shiites to desist from efforts to convert Sunnis to Shiite Islam and placed the blame for rising Shiite-Sunni tensions squarely on Iran.

"'Organized attempts by the minority sect to proselytize in areas where the other is dominant should stop, as part of mutual respect between the sects,' [the Union] said. 'The Islamic Republic of Iran should bear its responsibility to end sectarian strife.'"[2]

Online jihadis have seized upon the increased fear of Shiite influence. The Salafi Sunni al Qaeda members active on the web took advantage of the opportunity to raise such fears online, where verbal attacks and calls for violence against Shiite Muslims and Iran constantly appear in jihadi websites and forums.

As bombs and bullets flew between Shiite and Sunni militants in Iraq, and as Iran's nuclear program continued to frighten a number of Arab Sunni states, a new message appeared on the Muslm (spelled without an *i*) jihadi forum from a well-known source.

Iran and its associated Shiite sects are hijacking Arab causes and exploiting them to serve an expansionist scheme, a top Sunni Islamist cleric warned in a statement posted on the Muslm jihadi forum.

Sheikh Hamid al-Ali, based in Kuwait, is a leading Islamist ideologue whose teachings are often posted on Islamist websites. He has been linked to al Qaeda activities in the Gulf state and is described by the U.S. government as a terrorist facilitator who has provided financial support for al Qaeda–affiliated groups seeking to commit acts of terrorism in Kuwait, Iraq, and elsewhere. Ali is also well known for lashing out against Shiites.

In his statement, Ali cited Western reports tracking Iran's nuclear program and military expansion, before turning his attention to Iran's role in the region.

"'Lebanon is a vivid example [of] the Iranian expansionist scheme at the expense of real Arab causes, which are exploited by Shiite sects,' Ali said. 'Iran has also established strong relations with the Palestinian Islamic resistance, enabling it to use this relationship to organize events (in the Palestinian territories). Iran was very devoted to a Hamas victory in the elections.'"[3]

Ali called upon the jihadi movement to grasp the severity of the situation and become "aware of the reality of the size of Iran's influence . . . [we] must not allow Iran to exploit legitimate causes, as seen in Lebanon."[4]

Ali foretold of dark times ahead, saying the near future would be marked by "more isolation, friction, and escalation . . . and an inevitable confrontation."[5] A victory for Sunni Muslims is assured, Ali promised.

Responding to Ali's comments, members of the jihadi forum posted messages calling for holy war to be declared against Iran. "We ask that God makes the Islamic

State of Iraq declare war against Iran for the sake of Islam, and awaken the nation to the danger of Iran," one member wrote.[6]

Ely Karmon, a senior researcher at the International Institute for Counter-Terrorism (ICT), of the Interdisciplinary Center (IDC) Herzliya, placed the anti-Shiite hostility on display online in a larger context.

Citing an exchange of letters between the late al Qaeda leader in Iraq, Abu Musab al-Zarqawi, and Osama Bin Laden, Karmon said that al Qaeda had gradually come to accept Zarqawi's view that Shiites are infidels and represented a priority target for jihad.

"'This issue will dictate the Middle Eastern agenda in the years to come,' Karmon said. "In Iraq, al-Qaeda strikes Shiites every day. If the Americans withdraw, it will be presented as a Sunni victory, as Shiites hardly took part in the war against the Americans."[7]

The increasing hatred toward Shiites is in no small part generated by the virtual caliphate. Several Islamist Arabic-language forums are flooded with anti-Shiite and anti-Iranian messages, while the Muslm forum has even set up its own anti-Shiite online guide. In August 2007, one member described in a message his fantasy to see the Iranian embassy in Baghdad blown up by al Qaeda. A few days later, Iraqi police uncovered a bomb plot against the Imam Hussein mosque in Karbala, Iraq, the most holy site in Shiite Islam. Al Qaeda had repeatedly hit the site in the past.

A brief account of the origins of the Sunni-Shiite split is useful. During the founding days of Islam, in the decades following Muhammad's death in 632, a war broke out between claimants wresting for control over the new religion and state.

Following Muhammad's death, four caliphs—or rulers—successively took control of the new Islamic state Muhammad had founded. Only the last of them, Ali, was directly related to Muhammad, being his first cousin and husband of the prophet's daughter, Fatima. Ali took the reins of power after the third caliph, Uthman, was murdered at prayer. But after Ali assumed power, anger arose among Uthman's allies, which included Muhammad's powerful wife, Aisha, who accused Ali of not trying hard enough to apprehend Uthman's killers. Ali, Muhammad's sole living relative to succeed the Islamic state, was forced to step down, an act that so infuriated his followers that one of them murdered Ali for agreeing to forgo power.

Mu'awiya Umayyad—Uthman's cousin, the governor of Damascus, and an opponent of Ali—seized power and declared himself caliph, while Ali's younger son,

Hussein, agreed to put his claim to the caliphate on hold until Umayyad died. But when Umayyad passed away, his son, Yazid, took control of the caliphate.

Hussein and his followers waged war to retrieve the throne but were hopelessly outnumbered on the battlefield. They were massacred in a bloody battle in the Iraqi city of Karbala, which has since become one of the holiest sites for Shiites; they revere it as the site of Hussein's martyrdom.

Shiites hold that only Muhammad's descendants should rightfully rule the caliphate and lead Muslims. Shiite means partisans, short for partisans of Ali, and today they consider the Sunni ascendancy to the caliphate as one of the great historical injustices of the world. Sunni comes from the Arabic word *sunnah*, which means the words and deeds of Muhammad, prophet of Islam. Sunnis maintain that the first caliph, Abu Bakr, was the rightful heir to the Islamic state, while Shiites adamantly declare that Ali should have been the first, rather than the last, caliph and that Ali's bloodline should have continued to decide the caliphate's rulers. Radicals from both sides have continued this feud into the twenty-first century, in the physical world through thousands of bombings and shootings in Iraq, Afghanistan, and Pakistan; acts of torture and cruelty in Iraq; and in the virtual world, on the numerous Internet servers hosting the websites and the forums of the virtual caliphate dedicated to attacking and delegitimizing Shiites.

The Online Guide to Hating Shiites

The online anti-Shiite guide aims to prove "how Shiites pervert the Koran" and provides over twenty links to websites that demonstrate Shiite distortion of Islam's holy book.[8] This is a favorite theme among online anti-Shiite postings. If the world's estimated 290 million Shiites are following a defective version of Islam, then they must be classed as heretics and targeted for jihad, so the argument goes. Worse yet, the virtual caliphate accuses Shiites of plotting a sinister scheme to take over and destroy the true Sunni form of Islam.

"In the name of Allah, the all merciful, all compassionate," a prayer that precedes an anti-Shiite webpage reads. "There are many who are tyrannical and disbelieve in thee Allah, they light the fire of war. We act towards them with enmity and hatred until the Day of Judgement [*sic*], for Allah does not love mischief."[9] The quote is clearly directed against Shiite Muslims.

The webpage goes on to state that Shiite Iran has published Persian-language Korans filled with distortions of the original text. Scanned images of the offending verses were uploaded onto the website.

Other sections of the guide include a post headlined, "Shiite mothers attempted to assassinate believers in the messenger of Allah," an attempt to demonize Shiites. And yet another section is dedicated to an attack on the fervent Shiite belief in the Mahdi figure as a promised messiah.

The online guide provides a link to a webpage that claims that the founder of the Islamic Republic of Iran, Ayatollah Khomeini, said that "the Iranian people in modern times are better than the people of Hijaz during the era of the Prophet."[10]

Hijaz is the region in modern Saudi Arabia that contains the two holiest sites to Islam, Mecca and Medina. During the time of Muhammad, the people of Hijaz converted to Islam and helped found the first caliphate, or the first Islamic independent state, which subsequently grew into a massive empire.

Allegations that Khomeini would proclaim that modern Iran is superior in Islamic terms to the founders of the first caliphate is symbolic of al Qaeda's view of Shiites and Iran. They are perceived as usurpers who are attempting to supplant the true heirs of Muhammad and the founders of the twenty-first-century caliphate, the Sunni Muslim mujahadeen fighting the jihad.

Continuing with the guide, one section sure to upset the core sensibilities of Shiites contains several links to websites attempting to prove that "Shiites murdered Hussein."[11] To argue that Shiites were responsible for the death of their most beloved martyr is a surefire way to infuriate Shiite Muslims. The proof for the explosive claim is derived "from their own [Shiite] books."[12]

"Documents from the books of Shiites demonstrate that the Shiites are the killers of Hussein, may Allah be pleased with him," one link states, bringing readers to text that allegedly proves the damning charge.[13]

Another section of the guide brings Sunni readers to a webpage set up to mock Shiite beliefs. The section, titled "anomalies of Shiites," discusses with great hostility cases of sodomy among Shiites, with allegations that Shiites refuse to recognize sodomy as a crime.

Yet another section is dedicated to pointing out "the similarities between Shiites and Hindus," a true insult, as Hindus are considered by jihadis to be inferior, pre-Islamic idol worshippers who must be exterminated or converted through jihad.[14]

Shiites are often branded as Jews—a term synonymous with enemies of Islam in the radical Muslim lexicon. This accusation is often repeated, alongside an attack on the core Shiite belief of the Mahdi's return.

Son of the twelfth Shiite Imam and revered by Shiites, the Mahdi disappeared as a child and is alleged to be hidden from Allah's sight until the day of his return, during which he will herald a messianic Shiite golden age and destroy the Shiites' enemies in a massive war.

To link the Shiites' precious Mahdi figure to enemies of Islam is intended as an insult and a degradation. The guide goes to great length to link the Mahdi to the Talmud and the Jews.

"Other evidence on the characteristics of the Shiite Jewish Mahdi," the guide says:

> First: When the Jewish messiah returns, he will gather Jews from all corners of the Earth, to the place of their Jewish holy city, Jerusalem. When the Shiite Mahdi arrives, Shiites everywhere will meet him and go to the place of their holy city of Shiites, in Kufa.
>
> Second: When the Messiah leaves, dead Jews will return to life out of their graves to join the army of Christ [the authors of the guide confuse Christian and Jewish messianic beliefs here] and when the Shiite Mahdi leaves, dead Shiites will return to life and go of their graves to join the Mahdi camp. . . .
>
> The Jews tried all injustices to kill the messiah, like the Shiites tried every injustice to kill the Mahdi."[15]

The online guide reaches some outlandish and thoroughly illogical claims to back up its basic argument that Shiites and Jews are similar, and states that "Christ killed a third of the world's Jews, the Mahdi will kill two-thirds of the world's Shiites."[16] The guide continues to provide yet more "evidences and proofs," part of the indictment of Shiite Muslims as infidel agents worthy of being targeted for jihad.

And the campaign goes on. Everyday, new evidence of Shiite heresy and depravity will surface on the virtual caliphate's anti-Shiite section, in an obsessive manner.

"[The founder of the Islamic Republic of Iran, Ayatollah] Khomeini permits sodomy against wives and infants," a headline screamed across the Muslm jihadi forum.

The same post continued, "Khomeini said that the prophet Muhammad was unsuccessful in his call!" These statements attribute pure blasphemy and moral degradation to the founder of the Islamic Republic of Iran. The post's author even claimed his headlines were based on "a selection of speeches and letters of Imam Khomeini."[17]

"Khomeini accused the prophet, peace be upon him, of not conveying the message," another post headline said. The responses on the forum came fast and thick. "God curse this deviant to hell."[18]

Online jihadis are systematically turning up the hatred propaganda on Shiites and Iran, as incitement to violence against Shiites continues. One post placed on the Muslm forum was headlined: "Islamic State of Iraq bombs Iranian embassy in Baghdad, killing Iranian ambassador."

"For now it is a dream," the post's author wrote.[19]

13

Global Responses to the Rise of the Virtual Caliphate

Al Qaeda would not be in existence were it not for the pervasive presence of online jihadis. Western governments, media agencies, and analysts now begin a much-delayed response to this phenomenon. As they do, a number of urgent questions require their answers.

How can a collection of dedicated Internet sites spin a global web that has the power to convince middle-class Muslim youths, born in Western states, to sacrifice themselves for the purpose of killing their fellow citizens? How does content on a computer screen manage to send volunteer soldiers thousands of miles from home and undergo military training in order to take on vastly superior military forces and inflict serious damage on enemy armies?

These questions have greatly troubled Don Radlauer, a research associate who specializes in information technology at the International Institute for Counter-Terrorism (ICT), based at the Interdisciplinary Center (IDC) in Herzliya, Israel. The ICT is one of the world's leading counterterrorism studies centers and works with security officials and other centers around the world to pioneer new responses to terrorism.

In his attempt to understand what is taking place online, Radlauer takes an original approach. By examining the unique fusion of the Internet and the jihadi ideology that views human lives as sacrificial pawns for an ultimate cause, Radlauer believes that a new means is being used to fulfill an old objective. He defines that objective as the "switching off" of the basic human instinct to sympathize with other people in one's environment. This instinct is replaced with a desire to maim and kill people who have been objectified into demons.

"Let's just look at the Internet," Radlauer said during an interview with the author. "This massive, new thing only began its existence as we know it ten to thirteen years ago. It has spread very, very quickly, and as a new medium, it has got its own set of characteristics, which are still developing."[1]

In attempting to understand how the virtual caliphate works so efficiently, Radlauer homes in on the Internet's "combined social medium media," which he said "very easily leads to a process of radicalization." "If you try to mention an alternative opinion to the consensus held by users on a horse grooming website, the reaction and their rejection of your opinion sometimes resemble that of a religious cult," Radlauer pointed out, speaking from personal experience. "If something as innocent as a hobby can take on extremist tones online, what happens within political and ideological websites?"[2]

So what is it about the Internet that produces such an intolerant atmosphere? "The Internet is essentially placeless. If I start a singing group, I need to locate local singers. On the Internet, however, your neighborhood is the whole world. You can have very radical or unusual politics, and you can find people who agree with you very far away. The pressure to conform, to be mainstream, is gone," Radlauer stated.[3]

Once you establish close contact with like-minded people from around the world, anyone who enters your virtual realm with a different view could come under fire. A radicalization process has begun. Worse yet, the process is undetectable to those physically around you.

"If you're sitting at a desk at your computer, the people around you don't know what you're reading or writing. You could be dealing with the most extreme ideas, and there is no external sign of that whatsoever. There is no feedback to bring you back into the mainstream. This is dangerous—to live in a conceptual world which is isolated from the physical world, and one can drift into some strange waters," expressed Radlauer.[4]

The Virtual Caliphate and Immigration

According to Radlauer, the virtual caliphate has changed the entire nature of the assimilation of immigrants into their adoptive states. He seeks to understand why "people who grow up in a prosperous, Western democracy with no oppression" become jihadi terrorists:

> The whole nature of assimilation has changed. Once, people got off the boat, and all you'd get from your old country was the occasional letter. Once in a few years you could take a trip back, but the old culture was static and dead, and immigrants were immersed in the new culture. In America, for example, people enthusiastically become Americans. Now, an immigrant's old country is right there on their computer. The old culture is no longer static and dead. Children whose parents have assimilated can go back and revive the old culture. The pressure to assimilate has been tremendously reduced. In Britain, for example, many Muslims immigrants feel much less pressure to be British.[5]

Jihadis reach new pools of radicalized youths irrespective of physical border controls, thanks to their online presence. Specifically, it is the social dynamism of web forums combined with hard jihadi ideology that create such a potent mix. "The concern is that an Internet based on social groupings is likely to become the most important source of terror groups. No matter how much border control improves, terrorism based on the Internet itself threatens security."[6]

As stated previously, jihadis have created an online entity because there is no physical base to create the Islamic state, including and especially the Arab-Muslim states. If Radlauer's claim that the Internet can bring back the "old country" for Muslim immigrants is true, this revival should not, in principle, bring back plans to reconstruct the caliphate.

But the culture of Arab-Asian-Muslim states is, as seen in previous chapters, vastly different to the official government lines of those countries. Islamist political parties and underground jihadi cells are spread out across Egypt, Jordan, Syria, Saudi Arabia, Pakistan, and several other states.

Perhaps it is this culture from the old country that has been accessed by young Western Muslims, many of whom do not speak the language of their parents. English has become the lingua franca to discuss revived Islamic revolutionary ideas in the West.

During his investigation into the workings of the jihadi Internet entity, Radlauer has repeatedly found a shift taking place in the minds of the virtual caliphate's adherents, which, to his distress, turns out to be a lethal change and one that has taken place for as long as humankind has existed—with devastating results:

> Part of what terrorism is all about is the extreme end of the bell curve of alienation. Most people have feelings of empathy. They have enough imagination to empathize with strangers. They can see a stranger on the bus as a person who is going home to his children. The fact is, we need to do something to switch off the ability to empathize like that. The Germans during World War II were able to turn off the switch, so as not to see Jews as human beings. If the switch wasn't there, Hitler couldn't have turned it off.[7]

Today, that same switch is being turned off via the Internet in jihadi websites and forums:

> Terrorism is a manifestation of something frightening about human beings. Most individual serial killers suffer from an actual mental disorder. But as we have seen repeatedly, suicide bombers are perfectly sane. Most if not all Nazi concentration camp guards were sane. If we're going to fight terrorism, we've got to face the fact that we are dealing with human behaviour which is not unique in history.[8]

According to Radlauer, one of the most dangerous effects of the interaction between jihadism and the Internet is the resulting ability to demonize inhabitants of the brainwashed jihadi's physical surroundings. "The Internet allows people to suck themselves in. On the net, you're not constrained," the analyst said, underlining how the Internet allows individuals to "go crazy together" through a process of reinforcing delusions:

> People can get into mutual reinforcement, and once a group is formed, it becomes more extreme. Because your social life is more oriented around people on the Internet, it can be that much easier to objectify flesh and blood people around you, because your focus has become people on the net. Very close friendships can be formed among people who have never met in person, based only on Internet text messages, and this is going towards dangerous directions.

If you're getting your social strokes from people online, it is easier to dehumanize the people around you.[9]

The Virtual Caliphate—Fighting Back

Ron Radlauer offers an incisive view into the psychological and social dynamics that allows for individuals to alter their worldview and become radicalized. But the question of what concrete steps can be taken to counter the jihadi online entity remains open.

Evan F. Kohlmann, a U.S. terrorism analyst who has served as an expert witness in terror trials and has advised the FBI, argues that governments and militaries cannot act too soon in tackling online jihadis. "The United States is gradually losing the online war against terrorists," he wrote in a 2006 *Foreign Affairs* essay. According to Kohlmann, the U.S. government has been so preoccupied with fears of a "digital Pearl Harbor"—a dramatic online attack against vital national infrastructure or defense related websites—that it missed how the Internet has been mainly used by jihadis, to communicate with one another and organize themselves:

> To counter terrorists, the U.S. government must learn how to monitor [its] activity online, in the same way that it keeps tabs on terrorists in the real world. Doing so will require a realignment of U.S. intelligence and law enforcement agencies, which lag behind terrorist organizations in adopting information technologies. At present, unfortunately, senior counterterrorism officials refuse even to pay lip service to the need for such reforms. That must change—and fast.[10]

To be fair to the U.S. defense establishment, the American military does appear to have risen to the challenge, setting up a range of monitoring methods and eavesdropping on online jihadis. Israeli security agencies are also keeping a watchful eye on jihadi websites.

Until 2008 most counterterrorist agencies seemed keen on listening to the enemy. But in September 2008, something mysterious happened; a development that took about a month to hit the press. In October 2008, the *Washington Post* reported: "Four of the five main online forums that al-Qaeda's media wing uses to distribute statements by Osama bin Laden and other extremists have been disabled since mid-September, monitors of the Web sites say."[11]

To be clear, the websites in question fall under the ministry of foreign affairs category (see chapter 7). They are mainly used to retrieve messages from al Qaeda's leadership and send them to the outside world.

On September 10, 2008, one day before the ministry of foreign affairs announced that videos and new material celebrating September 11 would appear, four of these sites were taken off the Internet. On September 29, al Qaeda's central media dissemination service, the al-Fajr Media Center, claimed the sites "had disappeared for 'technical reasons,' and it urged followers not to trust look-alike sites."[12] Predictably, the sites' owners did not raise the white flag and worked hard to reestablish the forums on the Internet. According to the SITE Intelligence Group, one of the forums, al-Hesbah, came back online after twenty-four hours and carried with it al Qaeda's 9/11 celebratory video, the *Washington Post* reported.

"Is it like whack-a-mole when, if you close up one site, another site instantly re-appears? It would seem so," Steve Emerson, executive director of the Investigative Project on Terrorism (IPT) wrote in an e-mail to the author.[13]

During a major counterterrorism conference in Herzliya held by the International Institute for Counter-Terrorism in September 2007, a number of experts gathered to discuss the state of the international jihad today. One panel of professionals turned their sights on jihadi web activities.

Yigal Carmon is the president of the Middle East Media Research Institute (MEMRI), a high-profile service that translates Arabic media content into English, Hebrew, and many other languages. During the ICT's counterterrorism conference, Carmon, a member of the cyber jihad panel, said he thought that "what can be done is being done" in response to "the phenomenon of the internet jihad."[14]

"The Internet is America and America is the Internet," Carmon noted, adding that the majority of the telecommunications infrastructure making the Internet possible is based in the United States. Since "jihad websites are violating the regulations of Internet service providers [ISPs]," the response, which Carmon described as "simple and doable," is to approach those same ISPs and ask them to remove the websites.[15]

Because the ISPs were unknowingly hosting jihadi websites, Carmon maintained, there is no need for new legal frameworks to tackle jihadi websites, as the

ISPs usually remove the offending websites as soon as they are made aware of them. Carmon acknowledged that removing one website will result in it popping up elsewhere.

Approaching ISPs and asking them to remove jihadi sites is by no means an ineffective approach. Aaron Weisburd, interviewed for chapter 10, has been doing exactly that for years on his online vigilante website, Internet Haganah. Between 2005 and 2007, British authorities also took the same approach and have successfully removed the majority of al Qaeda–affiliated English jihad websites that formed the nucleus of al Qaeda's British indoctrination and recruitment drive. And yet, many of the same sites have resurfaced under new names.

In addition, many of the ISPs are not only based in the United States but spread out around the world, and a number of hubs of jihadi activity are in fact hosted in the Arab world. In theory, it should be easy to have them removed, as most Arab governments are even more threatened by the presence of such activity than Western states.

In September 2007, there was a recognizable drop in al Qaeda–affiliated Arabic-language jihadi websites, which have formed major online "street corners" for adherents of jihad. But such drops do not mean a decline of the virtual caliphate. They merely signal that the websites have "moved apartments" and will soon be operational again at a different web address.

For now, what is certain is that no system is in place to track down and shut down the thousands of websites composing the virtual caliphate. Al Qaeda's base on the Internet is more or less secure, for the time being, although the virtual base is becoming less and less secure as a safe haven. If one area of the web becomes uncomfortable, an easily made move is made to another region of cyberspace.

Perhaps the same websites that plot so much violence and project such hatred can also be used as invaluable windows into the jihadi world and provide a source of intelligence? No, said Carmon at the 2007 ICT conference. "None of the information we get from websites has ever led to a foiling of a terrorist attack," he declared.[16] His view is challenged by many. And new technology, currently being developed, will soon surface and give the virtual caliphate's enemies brand-new weapons with which to fight back.

14

Can the Virtual Caliphate Be Defeated?

The core question of whether counterterrorists can effectively bring down the matrix of Internet infrastructure, which makes the virtual caliphate possible, has a variety of answers, depending on whom one asks. It is a subject that is only now beginning to gain the interest of experts, itself a sign that the day the online jihadis presence will cease to exist is far off, if it ever arrives.

The first step to reaching an effective strategy for combating the online jihadi presence is to recognize that the battle is part of the physical war against jihadis, according to Dr. Maria Alvanou, an ITSTIME analyst. A part of Italy's Catholic University of Milan, the ITSTIME team deals with security, terrorism, and emergency management.

Can the virtual caliphate be defeated? "It depends on the online counterterrorism measures applied," Alvanou said in an e-mail interview with the author. "We must bear in mind the phenomenon of 'displacement' as we call it in criminology, meaning that jihadists can find either new ways in the net, or even employ completely different means not associated with the web. Fighting terrorism—as well as other types of criminal behaviour—must be done in a 'holistic' way and thorough way, fighting not only the symptom (internet use), but mainly the disease (root causes of terrorism activity)."[1]

What about the debate now raging between counterterrorism experts—is it better to shut down the websites or to view them as an indispensable window into the daily activities of jihadis? Alvanou wrote:

> Tough question. Again, what we know from fighting other forms of crime is applicable here. Combating a crime requires both intrusive measures and at times observing and intelligence gathering. The proper action of the counterterrorism authorities should be followed after judging each individual case. Timing is essential, maybe authorities can stop an attack and arrest the perpetrators—or it is more urgent to put down a site. Another very serious issue—though rarely put forward—is what kind of data and under what circumstances gathered can be admissible in a court? Because we have had cases for example in Italy, where data gathered by the authorities regarding the net activity of jihadists was considered inadmissible in courts and the accused were found innocent.[2]

Alvanou is not alone in claiming that today's legal systems are unequipped to deal with a hostile entity that exists in a virtual sphere. One American legal expert, discussed later in the chapter, proposes a legal overhaul to prepare the United States for the war against terrorist entities that seems set to define the first part of the twenty-first century. "Regarding governments, I would say they should update their legislation to be able to face the challenges of e-terror. Unfortunately, while on the technological level a lot has been done, legally we are really left behind and let's not forget, at the end of the day terror cases end up in court cases," Alvanou explained.[3]

Alvanou believes that the first step needed to bring governments and law enforcement agencies up to par for the battle against online jihadis involves far closer cooperation between various bodies. Governments must also be aware that national security should be defended with the most cutting-edge technologies: "Governments should use people in their law enforcement agencies that know technology! There is a need for cooperation between governments; we are talking about international terrorism on the net, so an international counter terror online strategy is needed." The private sector, where much of the technology and development of new concepts originate, needs to come on board and partner with governments' spy agencies and police forces for this grand effort. "Private corporations must be more alert on their controls. As for internet providers—they should really check what is going on in their servers and maybe there should be cooperation with counterterrorism authorities, in the sense that the latter can tell providers that there is an illegal use of their web server," she proposed, adding that "individuals must be encouraged to tip off the authorities if while surfing the net they encounter any terror-illegal activity. Freedom on the net cannot be considered as freedom for criminal activity."[4]

Alvanou has touched on some of the most important issues currently being examined by security agencies and governments that are needed in order to begin to cope with jihadis who reside on the web. Her next point, however, is the most crucial.

If the threat of terrorism is going to be significantly reduced in the world, the online threat must be recognized for what it is and placed as a top priority by governments:

> The internet is a very important tool for jihadists to recruit members, for communication of groups and even for gaining sympathy for their cause on a worldwide level. Since we are talking about international terrorism and the internet's help in a trans-national threat of jihadi terrorism, I would surely consider it a priority for the security forces to fight online jihad. The internet is both a means for the terrorism crime as well as its scene, and it is only logical that it should be under the very close inspection of any counter-terrorism authorities.[5]

The good news is that this recognition is beginning to happen. In a growing number of terror trials in the United Kingdom, suspects' Internet activities are being shown to courts. Damning Internet communications between members of a terrorist cell responsible for both the failed July 2007 Glasgow International Airport and central London car bomb attacks have been revealed during the trial process. Such developments are becoming the norm, rather than the exception.

In Israel, security forces have begun paying attention to Internet activities that could harm national security. In July 2008, for example, two Israeli Bedouins from the Negev town of Rahat were charged with plotting terrorist attacks via the Internet with al Qaeda members overseas and marking out civilian and military sites as targets. Their web activities were tracked by by Israeli security forces leading to a series of arrests in Israel in 2008. As with their UK counterparts, Israeli counterterrorism agents have followed the jihadis into the digital arena.

In the Ukraine in 2004, Vladimir Golubev, founder and director of the Computer Crime Research Center (CCRC), told a panel of experts that without international and interbody cooperation, the war against online jihadis could not be won.

"Nowadays cyber terrorism poses a peculiar social national and international threat that requires . . . Laws [that] should meet requirements made by modern technologies development. Law enforcement, special services and judicial system cooperation, their efforts... and their material security are the priority directions. None of the countries is [*sic*] able to prevent cyber crime independently and the international cooperation in this field is vital."[6]

The Technology—New Developments

Sending human agents to monitor the virtual caliphate is one way of keeping tabs on the enemy. In addition, however, computer scientists and programmers are taking their first steps in developing applications that are specifically designed to trawl the Internet and mark out the centers of the virtual caliphate. If these applications prove successful, the potential implications are exciting.

In June 2007, a number of computer programmers gathered from across the globe for a conference held at the Ben-Gurion University of the Negev in Be'er Sheva, Israel, to share their visions and innovations in this field. One such programmer was Nick Craswell, a researcher at Microsoft Research, Cambridge, Britain. Craswell laid out the principles for a search technology that can patrol the web. If configured correctly, the application could search for online terrorism activity.

Craswell's application included techniques for focused crawling—in other words, a systematic search of the entire Internet with a focus on certain subjects and keywords.

The application can be used to find and analyze connections between websites, Craswell said. The result, if such an application becomes available, would resemble a spotlight shone on the dark regions of cyberspace that are inhabited by the virtual caliphate, thereby allowing counterterrorists to map out its form.

Meanwhile, Gordon Cormack, a professor of computer science at the University of Waterloo, Canada, has been developing a computer model that allows for behavior prediction, he told conference participants.

Similarly, Mark Goldberg, of the Computer Science Department at the Rensselaer Polytechnic Institute (RPI), has been working on an approach to detect groups of online jihadis in a large social network that attempts to hide their communication. "Hiding groups may communicate regularly, during consecutive communication cycles, or in a streaming manner," he said.[7]

He proposed an algorithm that can pinpoint communications aimed at planning terrorist attacks and separate web chatter from background communication. The effect would be an Internet radar that can trace conversations between jihadis even when they attempt to camouflage their communications.

One of the most interesting presentations was delivered by Israeli information scientist Uri Hanani, whose company, MindCite Ltd., is working on "developing and implementing large-scale web-harvesting intelligent terror and security IT systems."[8]

Hanani said he was working on a system that would serve government ministries, domestic security agencies, and military agencies. Keeping the system as simple as possible to operate, Hanani outlined an idea that, if fully materialized, could be a highly sought-after program.

"First, like Google, it will crawl the web automatically in accordance to key words. And then it will harvest information through scanning databases, e-mail, whatever sources you like. What is important is the integration," Hanani said.[9]

"Before starting to work, we were forced to think about . . . someone paying a lot of dollars to put this system into place," he added. The result, as described by Hanani, sounds lucrative. "An online intelligence report is automatically prepared and done automatically at 5 a.m. When you come to office at 7, everything is ready. I wanted to produce a system that people are going to use."[10]

Hanani is not the only one working on an automated terrorism detection program. Researchers at the Department of Information Systems at Ben-Gurion University of the Negev are working on two exciting applications that could dramatically change the future of online counterterrorism operations.

The first project, the Multi-lingual Detection of Terrorist Content on the Web, has been created by researchers Mark Last, Alex Markov, and Abraham Kandel, the latter hailing from the Department of Computer Science and Engineering at the University of South Florida. Their idea is to create an application that can detect terror-related key words on the Internet and map out terror-enabling websites in a range of languages.

"Since the web is increasingly used by terrorist organizations for propaganda, disinformation, and other purposes, the ability to automatically detect terrorist-related content in multiple languages can be extremely useful," the computer scientists wrote. Using a new form of algorithm, "the results demonstrate that documents downloaded from several known terrorist sites can be reliably discriminated from the content of Arabic news reports using a simple decision tree."[11]

Thus, if the word "jihad" appears in the website of the Al Jazeera news network, the application would know not to include it in its terror web-activity tracking system. Only the appearance of the word "jihad" in an al Qaeda–affiliated website would show up in the system. In addition, the application can simultaneously search sites in different languages. In a promising first test of their program, the researchers report that the application has already worked in identifying terrorist websites in Arabic.

The computer scientists instructed their application to look at 648 web documents in Arabic—200 were from terrorist websites, such as Hamas's Palestinian Islamic Jihad, and 448 were from nonterrorist sites, such as Al Jazeera, Arabic CNN, Arabic BBC, and the United Nations website in Arabic.

Despite Arabic's unique grammar and frequent ambiguous meanings, the program successfully discerned between news websites and terrorist websites.

Over the past six years, the computer scientists expanded their team and developed a second project, called the Advanced Terrorist Detection System (ATDS). This project is "aimed at tracking down suspected terrorists by analyzing the content of information they access," its developers explained.[12] Such an application represents what is perhaps the ultimate answer to the virtual caliphate—using jihad websites against the jihadis who build and operate them.

"Governments and intelligence agencies are trying to identify terrorist activities on the web in order to prevent future acts of terror. Thus, there is a need for new methods and technologies to assist in this cyber intelligence effort," the computer scientists said. The first generation model of their solution, the Terrorist Detection System (TDS), operates in two modes: a training mode and a detection mode. After TDS learns to recognize normal web activity, it can then switch into detection mode, in which it "performs real-time monitoring of the traffic emanating from the monitored group of users, analyzes the content of the web pages accessed, and issues an alarm if the access information is not within the typical interests of the group."[13]

The researchers next developed what they hoped would be the next generation of TDS, and ATDS and reported encouraging results. "ATDS outperformed TDS significantly and was able to reach very high detection rates when optimally tuned," they stated.[14]

This time the aim is to identify terrorists and their supporters as they access terrorist-related information on the Internet. The way to track down terrorist suspects is by analyzing the content of information they access.

"ATDS should be able to detect terrorist related activities by monitoring the network traffic content," the scientists said; an analysis of purely text-based Internet content would do the job.[15] Conceptually, the idea seems simple enough to work: point ATDS at jihadi Internet content, and then track down the IP address of web surfers who are accessing it. A law enforcement agency can easily convert the IP address into a home address, and an investigation can be launched into who is accessing jihadi websites and why. An undercover investigation could lead to identification of a terror ring or of a radicalized web forum member at the beginning stages of a recruitment process.

"ATDS should be able to detect online suspected terrorists accessing terrorist related content. Such online detection may enable law enforcement agencies to arrest suspected terrorists accessing the web through public infrastructure such as public computer labs in a university campus or internet cafés. The detection result should include the suspected terrorist IP address," they explained.[16]

One of the most attractive features of ATDS is its ability to "monitor the network traffic without being noticed by the users or the monitored infrastructure provider," an ability its programmers describe as "passive eavesdropping." This is achievable by "installing an agent in the users' computers acting as a proxy."[17]

The programmers do not plan to stop there and have announced their intention to develop a more realistic model of the terrorist Internet user. "In addition, we are developing a cross-lingual version of the system as most terror-related sites use languages other than English (e.g., Arabic)."[18] Another planned upgrade will allow ATDS to analyze logos, pictures, colors, and other forms of images.

With such abilities, ATDS may well represent an excellent and effective tool for counterterrorists working to maintain their countries' national security.

15
The Gathering Counteroffensive

Since ATDS offers one way to combat the websites that make up the virtual caliphate, it is no surprise that such a solution has emanated from the private sector, according to Yael Shahar, director of the Database Project at the Institute for Counter-Terrorism (ICT) at Herzliya.

"Obviously, governments in areas affected by jihadi propaganda need to be aware of the dimensions of the problem and need to be ready to support those offering viable educational solutions. But the solutions themselves are most likely to come from the private sector," Shahar stated in an e-mail message to the author.[1]

At the same time, Shahar maintained that the ultimate answers will come from those who are most threatened by the virtual caliphate—"the Muslim populations of Europe, the US, and the moderate Muslim nations. These are the people who have the most to lose."[2]

The majority of Muslims living in the West, who do not affiliate with the jihad or support claims for the reestablishment of the caliphate, must rise up in dissent against the jihadis and make their voices heard online, too, Shahar advised. In fact, they have already begun to.

"So the short answer seems to be that in dealing with a social movement, what is needed is a grassroots response at the community and private sector level, which would then need to be supported, or at least receive the blessing, of governments. This grassroots response would obviously have to take its battle into cyberspace, using the same methods (chat rooms, forums, web-based education and debate) as the jihadis."[3]

Could this combination—made up of the private sector and a strong moderate presence on the web—be enough to turn back the tide of radicalism washing over the Internet? Shahar believes it can, to a certain degree:

> Does the West stand a chance in turning back the tide? I would say that the use of the internet for recruitment and propaganda is only a manifestation of a much deeper phenomenon. The question is, can the West turn back the tide on the advance of radical Islam in general? I would say that yes, it is possible to counter the jihadi propaganda on the net, though this is going to have to be a "bottom-up" campaign, waged mostly by non-governmental actors. There is no conceivable way to knock the jihadis off the internet completely—to censor them or take down their sites, etc. It is a matter of using the medium in the same ways as they use the medium, to target the same audience. The internet is a tool in this game, but it cuts both ways.[4]

All of the parties interested in combating jihadis can use the Internet in the same way as their enemies and disseminate rhetoric that counters the jihadi message. If the Internet is open to one party, it is open to others.

During a fascinating presentation at the ICT's Counter-Terrorism Conference in September 2007, Shahar discussed more innovative ways to weaken the virtual caliphate.

"The real problem with intelligence agencies is that they are becoming news agencies—they are being inundated by open source intelligence. What is intelligence? It is not today's news. Intelligence leads to an understanding of the enemy, to predictions (of their actions). There is good stuff on the internet for this," Shahar said.[5]

For counterterrorists looking at jihadis online, a wealth of information is accessible that can be used to determine divisions in the jihadi movement, pointing the way to weaknesses.

The jihadi movement's strategy, tactics, and structure are all visible online and are threatened by ideological splits, she explained. "How do we know this worries them? Because they say so," Shahar said, quoting an online statement by jihadi ideologue Sheikh Abu Baker, who said that "'there is concern that the momentum of the movement can be slowed by other clerics who challenge its legitimacy.'"[6]

"Jihadi ideologues are very open about what they fear," Shahar noted. And jihadis have many rivals to fear, including a popular, charismatic Saudi government cleric, Sheikh Rabee al-Madkhali, who has mocked and ridiculed Salafis. In light of such intelligence, rivalries can be exploited simply through striking up conversation on a jihadi forum. "Is there a possibility of a split? Why not play it up?"[7]

In an especially novel idea, Shahar suggested that security agencies make a "slight change" in the online recipes for bomb making that could lead to a premature explosion while the bomb is being prepared.[8]

The solution lies in tuning in, "not shutting down the sites across the board. Shutting down is counterproductive from our standpoint."[9]

"The [jihadi] people making policy are all online. There is no need for secret channels. We can learn from what they say, they've already done the work for us."[10]

The content of jihadi websites is partly written by senior ideologues themselves, Shahar pointed out, noting that "without the net there would be no global jihad."[11]

Shahar is not alone in saying that an attempt to shut down the virtual caliphate is unproductive, if not unrealistic.

Addressing the same panel, Dr. Katharina Von Knop, a researcher at the George C. Marshall European Center for Security Studies, offered a second innovative idea.

"Once al-Qaeda had one address—Tora Bora [Afghanistan]. Now they have thousands," Von Knop explained. One solution, she said, was to "create an international interagency intelligence system."[12]

Von Knop outlined a blueprint for creating a transnational database accessible to several governments, which would save intelligence agencies independently monitoring the same web channels countless hours in work.

"Eighty percent of [terrorism] data is open sources on the web. Several governments are analyzing the same websites, this is a waste of resources. One website is analyzed by seven to eight agencies, but instead, information can be shared," Von Knop argued.[13]

Von Knop has taken steps to realize this vision by creating a joint database of open source material. She believes her database will allow governments to amass the needed intelligence in order to decide on whether a jihadi website should be taken down or allowed to remain active.

Another solution, she said, was to produce "a counter-propaganda campaign on the web, to get users to hear a different message, especially when they are at the early stage of the radicalization process, when they have a chance to return to society. To run this, we need the support of imams and Muslim communities inside Europe. Leaders of Muslim communities don't influence young people anymore, only the radicals get to the youths."[14]

Professor Gabriel Weimann, author of *Terror on the Internet*, had a less optimistic outlook. Addressing the panel, he said, "We are far behind and losing the battle. The U.S. government has hired at least one thousand analysts. I know some of these students; they took Arabic courses. [But] the U.S. needs native speakers who know local dialects, who know the neighborhood."[15]

"International cooperation is a nice idea but it doesn't work. Most agencies in the same country don't cooperate," Weimann continued, pouring cold water on the idea. "This is a dynamic arena. We monitor them, they move. They respond to everything we do. It's an interactive war and we need a new army. We are years behind them, we have woken up too slowly."[16]

Attacking jihadi websites is futile in most cases, Weimann said; the Internet is simply too dynamic and liberal for such tactics to work. "If you hijack a website or block it, it will reemerge. [However], there is a lot you can learn by monitoring them," Weimann said.[17]

Reiterating a view expressed by others, the communications professor said one of the best solutions was to create an alternative online stage that would rival the Islamist message. "Jihadis never invented net technology. We can fight back, by appealing to the same population through a voice of peace, an alternative to death and suicide. The appeal should be made to the same target population."[18]

The debate above is a productive and interesting dialogue—albeit long overdue—between experts. It also shows, however, that experts are divided on what to do. Should the websites be monitored or destroyed? Can moderate Muslims create an alternative viable voice? Can governments really cooperate so they do not waste time dealing with the same online threats independent of one another?

Offering an alternative message on the Internet is certainly worth trying out. In fact, moderate Muslim religious leaders have already begun a counterassault on their jihadi rivals in chat rooms such as Paltalk, where extremists have spent so many hours. Other chat rooms have started opening with moderate voices, in which speakers have condemned the jihad and explained to listeners why jihadis have misconstrued and misunderstood the Koran.

The organizations calling for the caliphate to be reestablished are jihadi Salafis in nature, with a clear ideology. They powerfully argue that whoever does not share their goal of Islamic statehood is not a true Muslim. With this line of reasoning, they dismiss any moderate Muslim message on the Internet. Many such exchanges between moderate and radical Muslim web users have already taken place. We are far from knowing the outcome of this struggle, which is still at its beginning stages.

What if these jihadi websites formed a kind of state on the Internet—how would this state shape possible responses? It could create a far more focused and determined effort.

If Western governments concluded that they are at war with a virtual state that sends physical attacks in their direction, rather than mere nonstate terrorist actors that use the Internet to communicate, perhaps the incentives for international cooperation against online jihadis would grow.

If the technology and international cooperation proposed by the aforementioned experts develop to an extent in which the virtual caliphate is seriously challenged, then the entire global jihadi movement will face the threat of being seriously undermined. The jihadis' only claim to statehood, the virtual caliphate, will have been destroyed, and with it most of the movement's ability to function at all.

Time for a Legal Overhaul

The discussion of possible responses to the virtual caliphate is not complete without an examination of the legal frameworks that might be introduced to allow security forces to tackle the threat—with the full backing of their judicial systems.

A number of works, such as articles and research papers, have examined the struggle between the desire to maintain civil liberties and the right to privacy on the one hand, and the need to monitor nefarious communications traveling through the Internet to further the international jihad on the other.

In some sense, such a debate is irrelevant, because whatever stance a particular government takes on this issue will only apply to a fraction of the virtual caliphate. If the British government, for example, felt that it were entitled to intercept web communications within the territory of the United Kingdom, it would have access to only one portion of the borderless virtual caliphate—assuming it knew where to look. The jihadis can easily circumvent the British telecommunications infrastructure even while residing within Britain itself. Such is the nature of the Internet.

An international legal protocol would be a more relevant step, but only if a form of international intelligence sharing accompanied it, as proposed by Von Knop.

In the United States, despite the numerous, robust antiterrorism laws passed since the 9/11 attacks, "a new and deadly terrorist threat called cyber terrorism is now emerging that may, as many commentators predict, catch the United States totally off guard," wrote Jeffrey F. Addicott, professor of law and director of the Center for Terrorism Law at St. Mary's University School of Law in San Antonio, Texas.[19]

Addicott is concerned that a digital version of 9/11 could be in the works, or as some observers have described this scenario, a digital Pearl Harbor. "The same failure of recognition and lack of awareness prior to the terrorist air attacks of September 11, 2001, might be mimicking itself in the cyber world, and the attacks could prove to be more crippling and deadly than anything imaginable," Addicott warned.[20] Considering the modern world's level of dependency on computer databases, software, and the Internet, Addicott glances with worry at how cyber attacks can harm the infrastructures of water, electricity, banking, transportation, technology, agriculture, medical, nuclear facilities, waste management, and government services.

While some laws are already in place to aid governments in confronting the threat, much more reform is needed in America's legal system, Addicott noted.

He praises the USA PATRIOT Act for listing America's critical infrastructure but also points out that these are also at risk from cyber attacks. The PATRIOT Act singles out telecommunications, energy, financial services, water, and transportation sectors as having cyber components that require protection.

Beyond the familiar threat of cyber terrorism, web attacks can be used to inflict very real, physical damage. Addicott sketched an ominous scenario: "Those unfamiliar with the term cyber terrorism simply view the concept to mean an attack on the internet. This is far too simplistic a view," he wrote. Cyber attacks have the potential to destroy vital national infrastructure, he added, including defense systems and chemical plants.

Other potential targets include "water supply systems, transportation, energy, finance systems, and emergency services," Addicott continued. All of these infrastructures are managed by centralized computers called Supervisory Control and Data Acquisition (SCDA) systems, which make them vulnerable to cyberattacks if adequate safety measures are not put into place.[21]

Evidence exists to suggest that SCDA systems have already formed a target for jihadi plotters on the Internet.

A 2002 investigation by U.S. intelligence found that hackers based in the Middle East had studied SCDA computers that control electrical grids and water storage facilities in San Francisco, Addicott noted.

In a worst case scenario, hackers could hijack such systems and neutralize flood gates or seize control of powerful electrical generators, he said. In 2002 an Australian was arrested for hacking the SCDA of an Australian sewage and water treatment plant.[22]

While the PATRIOT Act granted government agencies the right to intercept web communications by terrorists, the punishments are still too weak, Addicott argued. The PATRIOT ACT has, however, clearly defined who is a hacker, as well as the electronic communications hubs that jihadi hackers seek to target. The PATRIOT Act is backed up by the Cyber Security and Enhancement Act (CSEA), which Addicott argued has "eased the warrant and subpoena requirements under the old Electronic Communications Privacy Act of 1986 (ECPA)."[24]

In the United States, the law has made a controversial shift toward granting increased rights to authorities in their war against the Islamist threat from the Internet, to the ire of civil rights and privacy campaigners. With America's traditional emphasis on individual civil liberties, this shift has sparked a heated debate.

Addicott believes the PATRIOT Act has provided America with "a valuable tool" to combat computer-savvy jihadis. But it cannot enable the government to meet the challenge head-on by itself. Funding and research must be increased dramatically if results are to be seen.

At the same time, legal reforms have not been accompanied by budget increases towards securing America's vital computer systems and infrastructure, he said.

Addicott joined the growing chorus of experts who are calling for collaboration between government and the private sphere to meet the challenge posed by online jihadis. "Unfortunately, the complacent habit of dealing only with realized threats has not imparted a sense of urgency that will ultimately be necessary to protect the cyber world," Addicott concluded.[25] The goal must be to ensure that the cyber world is as safe as the physical world.

16
The Virtual Caliphate's WMD Program

As governments, private corporations, academics, and intelligence agencies scramble to respond to the online threat, a race against time has begun. A base for the international jihadi movement already exists and may have taken the form of a virtual state. As this entity collectively attacks military forces and plots attacks on civilians in states standing in its way, sections of the jihadi online world are being used to prepare for a most sinister scenario: the use of a terrorist attack involving unconventional weapons, or weapons of mass destruction (WMDs).

Some security analysts hold the gloomy belief that such an attack—whether chemical, biological, or radiological—is inevitable and will strike a Western city.

One document available on several jihadi provides tips on surviving a nuclear strike. In an accompanying message, the authors note that they have extracted their instructions from an English manual and translated it into Arabic. The manual is preceded by this prayer: "And make ready against them all you can of power, including steeds of war to threaten the enemy of Allah and your enemy."[1]

According to the document's authors, enemies of the jihad will turn to WMD attacks out of frustration with the jihad's success, leading to a need to endow Muslims with the knowledge of how to survive such attacks.

"The main purpose of this booklet is to help individuals and families prepare plans to survive and protect themselves against the potential dangers of nuclear war in particular, and wars of mass destruction in general," the guide continued.[2]

"To escape nuclear attack is one of the most important topics of survival, applicable to nuclear, chemical and similarly genocidal wars, which the devout enemies of God would wage, if forced to find alternatives following their failure to implement their plans through initial use of conventional wars," the document added. "These have proven to be devastating failures at the hands of the black heroes of jihad and resistance to the occupation of Mesopotamia (Iraq)."[3]

Another, more worrying possibility is that as jihadis prepare to use a WMD on an "infidel" target, they have also begun to theorize how the targeted party could respond. If the targeted country responds with its own WMD counterattack, jihadis may have figured that the time has come to prepare for such a scenario.

"We ask God to grant us the ability to enable his rule across all corners of the earth," the document said. It was signed by "your brothers in the Jihad Media Battalion."[4]

Does Allah Permit WMD Attacks?

Do al Qaeda and its numerous tentacles and sympathizers around the world feel they have a religious mandate to use weapons of mass destruction? If one listens to security analysts and examines the details of botched terror attacks, the answer is in the affirmative.

In 2005 eight men were arrested in Sydney, Australia, for plotting to detonate a nuclear reactor. It is not difficult to image the carnage such an attack, if successful, could cause; a glance at the Chernobyl disaster would suffice. According to a Reuters report from that time, "their Islamic spiritual leader, also charged with terrorism offences, told the men if they wanted to die for jihad they should inflict 'maximum damage,' according to a 21-page police court document."[5]

In 2003, British police uncovered a plot to poison Londoners with the toxic agent Ricin. Court cases hidden from the media saw suspects confronted with evidence of their bomb-making efforts. These were tentative attempts to use weapons of mass destruction and demonstrate jihadi terrorists' unswerving belief in the legitimacy of using such means. There have been numerous reports of al Qaeda efforts to smuggle nuclear weapons into the United States, none of which have yet been verified publicly, while other reports talk of al Qaeda attempts to steal nuclear materials.

One of the most fascinating and potentially deadly conversations taking place at this time on jihadi Internet networks is a religious debate between proponents and opponents of WMD use.

In 2002 a number of al Qaeda clerics weighed in definitively on the issue. An article appeared on what was then al Qaeda's main website, al-Neda, which laid down the justification for killing no less than four million Americans.

Reportedly authored by Bin Laden's deputy, Ayman al-Zawahiri, and made available by MEMRI (the Middle Eastern Media Research Institute), the article is cited as saying: "We have not reached parity with them. We have the right to kill four million Americans—two million of them children—and to exile twice as many and wound and cripple hundreds of thousands. Furthermore, it is our right to fight them with chemical and biological weapons, so as to afflict them with the fatal maladies that have afflicted the Muslims because of the [Americans'] chemical and biological weapons."[6]

America, the message continued, understands only the language of force. A WMD attack is the only way to get America out of Muslims affairs, because "America is kept at bay by blood alone."[7]

For other jihadi thinkers, though, the price tag of four million casualties is not sufficiently high. In May 2003, an influential Saudi cleric and jihadi ideologue named Nasir al-Fahd ruled that infidels had killed ten million Muslims both directly and indirectly, and said that the killing of ten million infidels through the use of WMDs was therefore justified.[8]

The jihadica website, which monitors Sunni Islamist communications, states that Fahd turned to scriptural evidence in the form of the hadith to prove that jihadi soldiers can use WMDs—even if the enemy has not used such a weapon against Muslims.

Killing noncombatants unintentionally, burning the land and homes of the enemy, and inadvertently killing Muslims in a WMD attack are all acceptable, Fahd said, shortly before Saudi authorities imprisoned him.

Still, the damage was done, and Fahd's ideas have circulated repeatedly on jihadi web forums, infecting new minds with dreams of mass destruction.

In May 2008, around a year before he was killed, senior Pakistan Taliban member Beitullah Mahsoud declared in a video aired by *Al Jazeera* that Pakistan should activate its nuclear arsenal and use atomic bombs in the jihad.

"The problem of Pakistan is that it has lost what it used to have, and this is because it no longer has an independent political will, and its army does not adhere to its nuclear weapons. Moreover, it uses the weapons in its possession against the people and against the Muslims. Pakistan should use these weapons to defend the Muslims and to challenge the enemies," he said.[9]

President Barack Obama has not remained aloof to the threat. In April 2010, he called together an unprecedented international nuclear security summit, and delivered an explicit warning on the dangers of nuclear terrorism.

"Two decades after the end of the Cold War, we face a cruel irony of history: The risk of a nuclear confrontation between nations has gone down, but the risk of nuclear attack has gone up," Obama said. Jihadis would not hesitate to use nuclear weapons, he warned. "Were they to do so, it would be a catastrophe for the world, causing extraordinary loss of life and striking a major blow to global peace and stability."[10]

According to al Qaeda ideologues, a nuclear strike in the name of jihad would serve as a crushing preemptive strike, which could lead to a defeat of the United States, causing it to withdraw its forces from battle arenas in areas such as Afghanistan and Iraq.

Several jihadi clerics have issued online fatwas justifying the use of nuclear weapons, such as the one issued by Saudi cleric Sheikh Nasser Bin Hamed.[11] Made available in 2003, his ruling, "A Treatise on the Ruling Regarding the Use of Weapons of Mass Destruction Against the Infidels," is one of the first Salafi rulings on weapons of mass destruction. According to a MEMRI translation of the document, Sheikh Hamed believes it is "permissible to use weapons of mass destruction against 10 million Americans specifically, and against infidels in general, and that support for their use could be found in Islamic religious sources."[12]

The two-part document "discussed the legitimacy of the use of weapons of mass destruction within a particular time frame against a particular enemy...such as the case of America at this time," and forms a clear attempt to engineer a religious mandate to strike the United States using WMDs.[13]

> According to Sheikh Hamed, it is permissible to strike America with weapons of mass destruction in order to repay it in kind. As evidence, Sheikh Hamed cited three *Qur'an* verses: "If you desire to exact retribution, then adjust the penalty to the wrong you have suffered" (16:126); "Those whoso [*sic*] transgress against you, you may exact retribution from him in proportion to his transgression" (2:194); and "The recompense of an injury is a penalty in proportion

thereto" (42:40). After citing the *Qur'anic* verses, Sheikh Hamed wrote, "Anyone who looks at America's acts of aggression against the Muslims and their lands over the recent decades will permit this (the use of WMDs) based only on the section of Islamic law called 'Repayment in Kind,' without any need to indicate the other evidence."[14]

In line with this reasoning, Sheikh Hamed carries out a dubious casualty count of Muslims killed by the United States directly and indirectly, and reaches the number of ten million. "'With regard to the lands burned by their bombs, their means of destruction, and their missiles, only Allah can count.'"[15]

A weapon of mass destruction detonated on a target in America that would kill ten million people is therefore a legitimate recourse, Sheikh Hamed concluded. There is no need to produce any further evidence. "'Yet if we want to annihilate a greater number, we need further evidence.'" [16]

In the second section of his ruling, Hamed provides three pieces of evidence for the permissibility of WMD attacks. The first piece of evidence claims that Islamic texts justify nocturnal attacks on "'polytheists even if their offspring will be harmed by it.'" [17]

While Hamed concedes that Muhammad banned the killing of women and children, he worms his way out of the ruling by claiming that the Islamic hadiths show how Muhammad actually meant that only a *premeditated* killing of innocents was outlawed. "'But if their being killed is the result of a surprise attack and a raid, and an inability to distinguish among them (i.e. the enemy under attack) then there is nothing wrong with it, and the *Jihad* is not called off because of the presence of the women and children of the infidels.[18] Furthermore, the hadiths call for the burning of the enemy's land.

One hadith, authored by Ibn Omar, is extracted by Hamed as the second piece of evidence for WMD use. The hadith says Muslims must not shy away from any ploy against the polytheist enemy that succeeds in weakening their power and allows for the Muslims to conquer them. "'This *Hadith* includes clear evidence that it is permissible to burn the land of the enemy if the fighting requires it,'" he argued.[19]

Finally, for his third piece of evidence, Hamed turns to a hadith that sanctions the use of a catapult to strike an enemy city. Hamed skillfully works to convert a medieval religious ruling on war into a call to use unconventional weapons in the twenty-first century:

> It is known that the stone of the catapult does not distinguish between women and children and others; it is also (known) that it destroys any building or other thing that stands in its way. This constitutes proof that it is permissible to destroy the land of the infidels and to kill them – in the event that the *Jihad* requires this and in the event that the men of influence from among the *Mujahideen* think so – as the Muslims struck these cities with catapults until they were conquered and it does not say that they ceased and desisted out of fear that the infidels would be annihilated down to the root or that their land would be destroyed.[20]

With time, online calls to use weapons of mass destruction grew to the point that they became a chorus. According to a Jamestown Foundation report from 2005, al Qaeda has cleared the way to use CBRN (chemical, biological, radiological, and nuclear) weapons to further the goals of the global jihad.

Religious, practical, and strategic arguments have been laid down to back up this stance and ensure its acceptance among the ranks of holy warriors. "Departing from its previous reliance on in-house production and management of CBRN weapons, al-Qaeda is now encouraging other groups to acquire and use CBRN weapons with or without its direct assistance," according to the report.[21]

One al Qaeda operator and trainer, Abu Muhammad al-Ablaj, stated in 2003 that the use of sarin gas and nuclear weapons should be implemented. "They spared no effort in their war on us in Afghanistan and left no weapon but used it. They should not therefore rule out the possibility that we will present them with our capabilities."[22]

Later that year, Ablaj said chemical, biological, and nuclear weapons were a welcome strategic choice that would bring the crusader enemy to his knees with a plea for no further strikes—precisely the sort of "rationale" dismissed by the cleric Muhammad Abdul Qadir.

Most of the Ablaj's statements justify only reciprocal WMD use. But the Jamestown report also mentions a senior al Qaeda operative by the name of Mustafa Setmariam Nasser, who was forced out of Afghanistan following the 2001 U.S. invasion.

Away from the battlefield, Nasser spent years composing a guide for new jihadi soldiers based on his past experience. The 1,600-page document, called the Treatise of Strategic and Military Guidance, has a special sections on CBRN weapons.

The use of these weapons is "difficult yet vital," Nasser wrote, to ensuring victory. This is especially true in light of the ineffective results current jihadi tactics are achieving, Nasser added. It is incumbent upon the holy warriors to achieve WMDs either through purchasing them or by "producing primitive atomic bombs," by which Nasser referred to dirty bombs.[23] Jonathan Spyer, a senior Israeli research fellow at the Middle East Review of International Affairs (MERIA), says al Qaeda has reached a clear consensus over the issue. He identifies a clear desire among al Qaeda's leadership to obtain a nonconventional capability and cites the eleventh volume of al Qaeda's 5,000-page *Encyclopedia of Jihad* as being devoted entirely to methods by which chemical and biological weapons may be constructed. Renegade scientists are said to have cooperated with al Qaeda in obtaining such weapons, Spyer added.[24]

The Impending Threat

In August 2005, the SITE Institute, which monitors jihadi net communications, uncovered an online terrorist communiqué which included a map of the Washington DC subway system, and a proposal to carry out "an attack with chemical weapons upon this system to achieve 'amazing results.'"[25]

A chemical attack on an American subway system would achieve a "true effect" and would be worthy of comparison with 9/11, the message said.

One of the most dramatic examples of the online yearning for a radiological weapon can be found in a "preparation" document, teaching adherents how to prepare a dirty bomb. Similar documents have appeared on a number of jihadi forums.

In 2005 the Arab News reported that "a terrorist group has published a do-it-yourself plan to make a dirty bomb on its Internet site."[26]

One dominant member of the group, calling himself Abu Al-Harith Al-Sawahiri the Mujahid Sheikh, provided a virtual step-by-step guide on how to prepare a dirty bomb, beginning with tear gas canisters and working his way up to higher-grade bombs using uranium.

Gas bombs were another subject of detailed online tutorials by the forum member. "He introduces the subject by naming the different gases used for these purposes, and follows it up with their reaction with the elements, effects and their impact, before concluding by telling all where to buy them," the Arab News explained.[27]

"The writer goes on to give lessons on how to prevent and or cure oneself if exposed to such gases, until he is asked by one of the participants in the Net forum to give a lesson on how to make gas bombs from scratch and from easy-to-get substances. Al-Sawahiri promised his fellow 'Mujahedeen' that he would teach them how to make the lethal gas phosgene and how to use it," the article added.[28]

Despite the existence of some isolated internal resistance to a WMD terrorist attack, there can no question that online jihadis are working to prepare al Qaeda's soldiers for a mass casualty strike against an unspecified target.

The outpouring of manuals on how to create chemical and dirty bombs means that any religious qualms about carrying out such an attack have long been settled.

If a WMD terrorist attack can be traced back to any territory, a massive response and possible land invasion of that area seem likely results. Nevertheless, all of the signs from the virtual caliphate on this issue are sobering. The Internet is being used to call for and plot nonconventional attacks.

17
Future Scenarios

No one could have predicted the possible existence of the virtual caliphate roughly fifteen years ago, and today it is difficult to foresee how this phenomenon will continue to develop. This chapter will detail three possible scenarios. Some possibilities seem more likely than others, but history has often shown that the most unlikely tend to become reality.

Scenario 1 Caliphate: From virtual to physical

The first scenario is that the virtual caliphate attains its stated goal and successfully catapults the international jihadi movement into a real-life physical Islamic caliphate state. The following fictitious news report gives a taste of this scenario.

> Baghdad—After years of bloody conflict with jihadi insurgents, President Barack Obama has ordered American troops to vacate Iraq, completing a gradual troop withdrawal program. Despite much American success in fighting al Qaeda, the Iraqi state propped up by American troops collapsed soon after the exit of U.S. troops from the country. Al Qaeda forces converged on Baghdad and Sunni areas in central Iraq, declaring the establishment of an Islamic state.
>
> Here's how al-Qaeda leaders might respond to such a development: "This is a momentous day for the mujahadeen," declared al Qaeda deputy Ayman al-Zawahiri. "I now call on our victorious brothers in Iraq to declare an Islamic caliphate in the Land of the Two Rivers and realize the dream that the Muslim nation has been yearning and struggling to achieve for so many years. Our

victory over the world's strongest power demonstrates that no force can beat an Islamic army, fighting to establish Allah's rule on earth."

Al Qaeda leaders in Iraq soon followed with an audio statement released on dozens of jihadi websites simultaneously. "Today, Allah has chosen to reward the Muslim nation with the reestablished caliphate," one said in the recording. "I call on all mujahadeen everywhere in the world to come to the Caliphate of Iraq and defend its borders from the treacherous Persian Shiite forces now amassing to attack our state. The Caliphate of Iraq will have the Koran as its constitution. I call on all Muslims everywhere to support our Caliphate and to urge their governments to send us aid. If the so-called Muslim governments refuse to help, let the Muslim people rise up and overthrow them. Let them spread the borders of the caliphate to cover the face of the Muslim lands."

The nascent Islamist state came under immediate attack by Iraqi Shiite militias backed by Iranian Revolutionary Guards units, as the two sides traded missile fire. The area that once formed Iraq has witnessed millions of Shiites stream out of greater Baghdad and its surrounding areas, with thousand reported killed as they tried to escape the newly formed caliphate state. Following an emergency session, the UN Security Council has called on the world to "refuse to recognize this entity" and asked Muslim and Arab leaders to denounce the newly established state. Egypt has declared martial law as thousands of Islamists marched through Cairo's streets calling for an Islamic revolution. Meanwhile, Saudi Arabia has placed its military on heightened alert following threats by the Caliphate of Iraq to strike against what they described as America's stooges and usurpers of Mecca.

If a physical caliphate is ever established, its birth may well resemble the events described above. If the caliphate is born in the Sunni areas of Iraq and survives the likely Shiite onslaught, the Iraqi caliphate would become the new world center of jihadis, who would do their utmost to keep their state in existence. The various ministries described in the preceding chapters would take physical form and be housed in government buildings—a ministry of war, Islamic moral affairs, foreign affairs, and so forth. The virtual caliphate would be replaced by websites calling for support of the Iraqi physical caliphate, as the virtual state would take on a physical form.

Many of these hypothetical situations could ensue in the event that jihadis reestablish a state in Afghanistan.

Although the Internet would still be used to spread procaliphate propaganda and recruit aid, the array of websites that fulfill the role traditionally reserved for the government of a state could vanish. Instead, the web could be used to maintain the Iraqi or Afghan caliphate and to seek its expansion. Alternatively, the virtual components of the caliphate would remain in place in order to bolster the physical caliphate.

Scenario 2: Counterterrorist Agencies Disable Virtual Caliphate

From the outset, it must be stated that this scenario is by far the least likely to materialize. Again, the situation is theorized by a fictitious news report.

> Senior law enforcement officials and representatives of hi-tech firms held a celebratory joint press conference today to announce a drastic drop in online terrorist activity, following the successful launch of Project Takedown.
>
> A joint cooperative of leading technology firms, computer scientists, and international law enforcement agencies, Project Takedown was launched last year using an ultrapowerful web application that identifies the majority of operational jihadi websites. Unprecedented cooperation between several governments allowed information on the websites to be stored on a joint database.
>
> "Within days, we had placed a marker on the majority of jihad websites," the project's director told reporters. The application then installed Trojan horses on the home computers of jihadi forum users and crashed the servers storing jihadi websites. Since then, the application has continually trawled the web, automatically destroying the newly emerging jihadi websites as they attempt to resurface.
>
> "This is the first time authorities have succeeded in controlling the Internet," the director said, adding that civil liberty groups need not be alarmed as the world's law enforcement agencies "will only unleash this application against the websites that call for the murder of innocents in the name of a murderous ideology."
>
> "Once the technology became available for marking out terrorist websites, we concluded that it was better to take them down rather than use them to

> eavesdrop on the enemy. Who knows how many lives we have saved by taking steps to preemptively avoid the brainwashing of youths," he emphasized.
>
> Project Takedown's next task is to continue to monitor the web and prevent any reemergence of jihadi forums. "Having obtained this enormous goal, we expect the level of global terrorism to drop dramatically," its director predicted. "Al Qaeda will find it much more difficult to train and mobilize recruits around the world."

The scenario described above is clearly the least likely to come true. The technology for such an application is currently in its infancy, and no application to date has been able to exert any form of total control on the Internet. Computer scientists are taking their first steps in developing applications with such capabilities. Meanwhile, security and intelligence firms have shown little interest in cooperating with one another or sharing information on jihadi sites.

Scenario 3: The Middle Road

As things stand, the phenomenon I have described as the virtual caliphate will likely continue to exist, though its future seems slightly less secure, as technology is being developed to enable counterterrorists and governments to fight back.

But jihadis are highly innovative and will no doubt employ their own techniques to develop countermeasures, a process we have already with the appearance of an al Qaeda encryption system. It is naïve to believe that the virtual caliphate can be destroyed, though it can certainly be damaged.

While some sort of independent Islamic entity may well be declared somewhere such as Iraq or Afghanistan, it could still be a far cry from the dream of a full-blown caliphate, leaving the virtual version of the Islamist state with a reason to continue to exist.

Events on the ground will largely be guided by the virtual caliphate's status on the Internet. A healthy and unchallenged virtual caliphate will mean many terrorist threats and a well-organized, well-numbered, highly motivated global jihadi movement, fully interconnected. Terrorist attacks can easily be planned and directed through the virtual caliphate's ministries, while the jihadi movement would appear strong as the propaganda continues to draw in vulnerable youths. Threats would continue to be issued to governments and civilian populations, and the war declared by jihadis on the rest of the world could last for decades.

A weakened virtual caliphate would result in a decrease in ability by al Qaeda and its associates to replenish troop levels, spread propaganda, and organize themselves. Even its loosely structured cell system would suffer, as members would not be able to communicate as effectively or be activated with ease.

The control of online Salafi self-pronounced clerics over the daily lives of the virtual caliphate's inhabitants would decrease and with it the radicalization of some Western Muslim youths would occur.

"If Allah Wants an End, He Will Create It"

As far as the clerics of the virtual caliphate are concerned, the future could not be brighter. An e-book (originally a lecture) available from the British jihadi site, IslamBase, called "Allah Is Preparing Us for Victory," was composed by Imam Anwar al-Awlaki, a young American cleric with Yemenite origins, arrested in Yemen because of his jihadi activities.

Awlaki has a simple message for his followers: the victory is assured, simply keep fighting. "If Allah *'Azza wa Jall* wants victory for this *Ummah*, then Allah *'Azza wa Jall* creates the circumstances for that. So you can sense victory is coming by looking at what is happening today," Awlaki declared.[1] The earth will be inherited by the pious, he included.

The current era has seen disbelievers attempting to "extinguish the light of Allah. . . . They are trying to stop the flow of Islam and Allah *'Azza wa Jall* says they will fail. When we look at the amount of money they are spending on fighting Islam it is amazing; and you think about how much Allah *'Azza wa Jall* has given them (i.e., the *Kafireen*), and how many resources are under their hands; and they spend all of this to fight Islam!"[2]

The infidels may control "every powerful media outlet on the planet," the governments, police forces, and the entire planet, but this is no time to be despondent, Awlaki said with optimism.[3]

A verse from the Koran has predicted these developments, he said. "'They will spend it, then it will become anguish for them, then they will be defeated.' (*al-Anfaal*: 36) So let them spend their money as that's how they will be defeated."[4]

Hence, holy warriors should be joyous over the massive advantage in resources at the hands of their enemy, as this is what has been prophesized. All of these factors add up to one truth, Awlaki said. "Victory for Islam is soon; victory is on its way."[5]

When a human power wages war against the divine, Awlaki maintained, the outcome is clear. "It's not the Muslims who are waging war against them, it's Allah *'Azza wa Jall*! America is in a state of war with Allah *'Azza wa Jall*! 'Allah has promised, to those among you who believe and work righteous deeds, that He will, of a surety, grant them in the land, inheritance of power, as He granted it to those before them.'"[6]

Awlaki struggles to understand why anyone should doubt that the caliphate will be reestablished. "*Khilafah* [caliphate] will be given to those who have *Iman* [belief] and practice. . . . Muslims are now in a state of fear. Allah is promising us here that He will give us security. Allah *'Azza wa Jall* has promised this *Ummah*: *Khilafah*."[7]

This sort of historical determinism is on display across the virtual pulpits of the virtual caliphate.

Clerics place our current time into a slot right before the reestablishment of the caliphate. This messianic belief is partly based the following hadith, eagerly cited by Awlaki:

> "The Prophethood will last among you for as long as Allah wills, then Allah would take it away. Then it will be (followed by) a *Khilafah Rashida* (rightly guided) according to the ways of the Prophethood. It will remain for as long as Allah wills, then Allah would take it away. Afterwards there will be a hereditary leadership which will remain for as long as Allah wills, then He will lift it if He wishes. Afterwards, there will be biting oppression, and it will last for as long as Allah wishes, then He will lift it if He wishes. Then there will be a *Khilafah Rashida* according to the ways of the Prophethood," then he kept silent.[8]

The prophecy describes perfectly what is taking place now, according to Awlaki. Muslims are currently at the second-to-last stage, that of "biting oppression," just before the reestablishment of the rightly guided caliphate.

"Sometimes we complain about our times, that we are living in the worst times —the *Ummah* is weak, the *Ummah* is defeated and disunited, we wish we were living in . . . times of the heroic Islamic eras," Awlaki said, drawing on the fears of his followers.[9]

But the situation faced by al Qaeda today is the same as that faced by Muhammad and his companions fourteen centuries ago. "When the *Sahabah* [Muhammad and his companions] came, they fought entire surroundings including the two super powers—the Persian Empire and the Roman Empire—and all the Arabs around them that were against them. And this is similar to our situation today and this wasn't the case in our history before."[10]

All of this amounts to one very exciting fact for Awlaki: "The mission of the people today could be very great. We are not saying it is equal to the mission of Muhammad and his companions, but it is going to be very great."[11]

Victory is around the corner, and the victorious group al Qaeda has launched its campaign, and a radicalized interpretation of Islam will dominate the world through the caliphate, the cleric assured.

The time is near, the solution simple, and the cause divine, the cleric told online readers triumphantly. The worse things appear, the better they actually are. From a counterterrorist perspective, there can be no worse an enemy than one who does not know he has been defeated.

18
Virtual Statehood?

The Islamic State in Iraq released online a list of names of Sunni tribal leaders in Iraq that it intends to assassinate. Their crime: cooperation with American forces and the Iraqi government. On the one hand, this development may signal an increased fear by al Qaeda in Iraq, a fear based on the failure of their message of jihad to reach the target audience of Sunni Muslims. In response, the virtual caliphate's ministry of war is activated to seek out targets and intimidate others into compliance.

On the other hand, the announcement may also signal the possibility that the day is growing closer when a caliphate in Iraq is announced. The release of the hit list resembles that of a totalitarian government zealous to annihilate internal opponents, and al Qaeda in Iraq has already assassinated Sunni leaders guilty of working with the Americans in an effort to stabilize the country.

Either way, the release of such a hit list on the web, and the subsequent attention it received in the world's press, has allowed the jihadi movement to project a more powerful image.

This in turn could push a larger number of Muslim youths to turn to the virtual caliphate's indoctrination and recruitment centers. Some of them will then be afforded online training in bomb making and operating other weapons, and will then be placed into jihadi cells.

These cells will then either be activated for a martyrdom operation anywhere in the world or join the ranks of the soldiers fighting frontline battles with infidel armies. Their actions will be idealized and form propaganda materials that will be used to hook more youths.

The terror and fear caused by their actions will allow the virtual caliphate's ministry of foreign affairs to issue threats to enemies and embolden jihadis to influence democratic elections or the decisions of governments. The goal of forcing Western militaries to abandon areas such as Iraq and Afghanistan will remain fixed. If achieved, jihadis will declare a reestablishment of a physical caliphate, and a new and more dangerous center of international jihad will be formed.

The chain of interconnected events described above provides a glimpse into the inner dynamics of the virtual caliphate. A successful action by one ministry has a domino effect and empowers the whole entity. The benefiting party, the global jihadi movement, will then feel it is one step closer toward achieving its goal.

And it is this goal, the caliphate state, that may already have come to fruition on the Internet, whether the jihadis declare so openly or not. For it is only on the Internet that call after call is made for the establishment of this state, as made by Abu Hamza al-Masri, the radical cleric currently serving a seven-year prison sentence in Britain. Masri may be behind bars, but his words continue to reach a number of British Muslim youths through a jihadi website.[1]

In an online document called Allah's Governance on Earth, Masri outlines a prophecy that the caliphate is around the corner.

The Hizb ut-Tahrir website in Britain continues to dream of the caliphate. "80 years on from the destruction of the Khilafah the forces of Shaytan still continue to divide and disunite the Ummah."

"The Aqeeda [path] of Islam inherently unites Muslims. The only thing stopping it is a courageous leader who stands up calling for the unity of the Ummah. This leader will not emerge, brothers and sisters until we make the establishment of the Islamic Khilafah the single most important issue in our lives."[2]

In August 2007, Hizb ut-Tahrir organized a conference at Alexandra Palace in London, inviting influential speakers from around the world to address thousands of listeners on only one topic: how to found the caliphate as quickly as possible.

Hizb ut-Tahrir's website said thousands of people attended the conference. Countless more can attend online through Hizb ut-Tahrir's website, which has uploaded the lectures in audio format.

The leader of Hizb ut-Tahrir in Britain, Jalaluddin Patel, said in his speech that the call for the establishment of a global Islamic state "holds currency on the streets of Cairo, on the streets of Karachi . . . and on the streets of Tripoli. And indeed in almost every city in the Muslim world."[3]

"Brothers and sisters, ladies and gentlemen, plans are being made east and west . . . for this Muslim world," Patel declared. "We from Hizb ut-Tahrir believe passionately that true liberation will come to the Muslim world when we dispense with these ruling elites and these western-inspired systems, and in their place we establish Islam through state and society. Islam solves each and every problem that the Muslim world faces today."[4]

Abu Shaker, an activist from Hizb ut-Tahrir in Lebanon who has tangled with Lebanese security forces, also addressed the conference.

"Next week marks the 83rd anniversary of the collapse of caliphate, that unprecedented tragedy in the history of mankind where the Islamic way of life came to a halt, a halt that we believe is only temporary one. We look forward to the rising new dawn of Islam," he said.[5]

The caliphate will be the perfect state, its planners and would-be architects promise Muslims the world over.

The Internet is not merely being used by jihadis to communicate or propagandize. It has become a transport vehicle for a homeless, lethal movement. If the existence of a virtual Islamist state, with discernible ministries and functions, can be confirmed, its recognition would mark a paradigm shift in the way people organize themselves, shape their identity, and form social, political, and religious bonds.

The marriage between a movement seeking to go centuries back in time and the most cutting-edge communications technology could very well signal a new era in history, one in which geographic boundaries marking out states have become less relevant.

Newly recruited jihadis in Britain, Saudi Arabia, or North America share a common bond with one another more so than they do with their next-door neighbors and fellow citizens.

Online members of the virtual jihadi presence could be said to share a common identity, perception of history, and sense of destiny. Many of these attributes are the hallmarks used by political scientists to determine the existence of nations. The virtual caliphate might be described as the borderless nation-state of jihadis.

The People Behind the State

The virtual caliphate could not exist without the legions of online jihadis who breathe life into it, groups that many terror specialists believe are growing at this time. This story of the virtual caliphate is really the age-old story of people who fall under the belief that they are God's soldiers. Among other things, the preceding chapters have described what happens when human beings decide to eliminate viewpoints they do not share.

In many ways, the virtual caliphate is the latest manifestation of religiously motivated fanaticism, an affliction that has plagued humankind since the beginning of recorded history.

At the same time, a number of formally radicalized jihadis have renounced their affiliations, as growing numbers of moderate Muslim religious leaders find the courage to tackle the Salafi movement. And the moderate voices are growing louder and stronger by the day. They are the most likely party to deliver a death blow to the jihadi movement, online and off, someday.

For now though, the struggle is far from over, as new clerics are taking the caliphate's message forward through the Internet. Sheikh Omar Bakri Muhammad, whose audio broadcasts declaring war on Britain appeared at the start of this work, continues to reach English-speaking Muslims through the web. For instance, his book, *The Road to Jannah* (paradise), uploaded onto the Internet, chimes in with the caliphate message:

> The call for the establishment of the caliphate echoes all around the Muslim and indeed the non-Muslim world today. . . . The Muslims have understood that the murder, rape, pillaging and poverty that exist today do so because of the lack of implementation of Islam. . . . The Muslims of today are working to culture the Muslims to speak to the people of power and to ultimately make that breakthrough that will lead to the establishment of the caliphate. In their minds they have their eyes on accomplishing the feat that the Prophet and his companions achieved.

It is difficult to fight a war against the enemy who believes God is his commander. The scope and power of the virtual caliphate is testament to the determination that religiously motivated warfare imbues.

For now, the world is forced to accept the presence of such a dangerous entity on the Internet. Today, the virtual caliphate is an alliance of holy warriors who are never farther away than the click of a mouse.

Notes

Chapter 1: The Strangers

1. Terrorists Take Recruitment Efforts Online, 60 Minutes, CBS News, March 4, 2007, http://www.cbsnews.com/stories/2007/03/02/60minutes/main2531546.shtml.
2. Abdel Bari Atwan, "Total war: Inside the new Al-Qaeda," *Sunday Times*, February 26, 2006, http://www.timesonline.co.uk/tol/news/article735058.ece.
3. Omar Bakri Muhammad, online sermon, Paltalk chatroom; see also sections of the sermon in Sean O'Neill and Yaakov Lappin, "Britain's online imam declares war as he calls young to jihad," *Times* (London), January 17, 2005, http://www.timesonline.co.uk/tol/news/uk/article413387.ece.
4. Ibid.
5. Ibid.
6. Ibid.
7. Ibid.
8. Ibid.
9. Yaakov Lappin, Analysis: War declared on Britain, *Ynetnews,* July 7, 2005, http://www.ynet.co.il/english/articles/0,7340,L-3109521,00.html.
10. Sean O'Neill and Yaakov Lappin, "Britain's online imam declares war," *Sunday Times*, January 17, 2005, http://www.timesonline.co.uk/tol/news/article413387.ece.
11. O'Neill and Lappin, "Extremist Islamist."
12. Gary R. Bunt, *Islam in the Digital Age: E-Jihad, Online Fatwas and Cyber Islamic Environments* (London: Pluto Press, 2003), 198.
13. Ibid.
14. Reuters, "Qaeda wants Saudi king killed over interfaith call," July 28, 2008, http://uk.reuters.com/article/idUKL848592220080728.

15. Al-Ghurabaa, online jihadi video, www.ghurabaa.co.uk (site now discontinued); an altered version of the video can be found at http://www.youtube.com/watch?v=TjzxYdbiLk4&feature=related (accessed July 28, 2008).
16. Ibid.
17. Ibid.
18. Ibid.
19. Ibid.
20. Ibid.
21. Ibid.
22. Ibid.

Chapter 2: The Roots

1. Abdullah Azzam, *Defense of the Muslim Lands: The First Obligation after Iman*, trans. Brothers in Ribatt, http://www.religioscope.com/info/doc/jihad/azzam_defence_2_intro.htm.
2. Ibid.
3. Ibid.
4. Ibid.
5. Ibid.
6. Ibid.
7. Juan José Escobar Stemmann, "Middle East Salafism's Influence and the Radicalization of Muslim Communities in Europe," *Middle East Review of International Affairs* 10, no. 3 (September 2006), http://meria.idc.ac.il/journal/2006/issue3/jv10no3a1.html#bio.
8. Ibid.
9. Ibid.
10. Abu Hamza al-Muhajir, Internet message, Caliphate Voice Channel, http://cvc-online.blogspot.com/ (accessed November 20, 2006; site now discontinued).
11. Ibid.
12. Azzam, *Defense*.
13. Ibid.
14. Ibid.
15. Ibid.
16. Ibid.
17. Ibid.
18. Ibid.
19. Ibid.

20. Sayyid Qutb, *Milestones*, http://majalla.org/books/2005/qutb-nilestone.pdf.
21. Ibid.
22. Ibid.
23. Ibid.
24. Ibid.
25. Ibid.
26. Ibid.
27. Ibid.
28. Ibid.
29. Ibid.
30. Ibid.
31. Ibid.
32. Ibid.
33. Ibid.
34. Ibid.
35. Osama Bin Laden, background and declaration of war, http://www.terrorism-files.org/individuals/declaration_of_jihad1.html.
36. Ibid.
37. Ed Husain, *The Islamist: Why I Became an Islamic Fundamentalist, What I Saw Inside, and Why I Left* (London: Penguin, 2007), 83.
38. Ibid., 84.
39. Ibid., 89.
40. Ibid., 95.
41. Ibid., 95.
42. Trevor Stanley, "Understanding the Origins of Wahhabism and Salafism," *Terrorism Monitor* 3, no. 14 (July 2005), http://www.jamestown.org/programs/gta/single/?tx_ttnews%5Btt_news%5D=528&tx_ttnews%5BbackPid%5D=180&no_cache=1.
43. Ibid.
44. Ibid.

Chapter 3: Going Online

1. *Islamic Revival*, Volume nine, March 7, 2006, http://www.khilafah.com/home/category_list.php?&category=Khilafah+Magazine&offset=0, March 7, 2006. (accessed May 16, 2006).
2. Ibid.
3. Ibid.
4. Ibid.

5. Ibid.
6. Al-Ghurabaa, online jihadi video, www.alghurabaa.co.uk (site now discontinued).
7. *Islamic Revival.*
8. Ibid.
9. Ibid.
10. Sermon by Jamaal ud-Deen Zarabozo, "fighting to establish an Islamic state," Muntadaa Forum, http://Muntadaaa.aswj.net//index.php?showtopic=3988 (accessed November 20, 2006).
11. Ibid.
12. Ibid.
13. http://globalmbreport.com/
14. Ibid.
15. Ibid.
16. Ibid.
17. Ibid.
18. Aaron Weisburd, e-mail message to author, July 26, 2007.
19. MEMRI Blog, "Mujahideen Secrets," http://www.thememriblog.org/blog_personal/en/239.htm (accessed January 17, 2007).
20. Ibid.
21. Ibid.
22. Ibid.

Chapter 4: The Ministry of War

1. Al-Ghurabaa, "The Islamic Conquests to Spread Islam," www.alghurabaa.co.uk (site now discontinued).
2. Ibid.
3. Ibid.
4. Abu Baraa, online sermon, Paltalk chatroom, February 13, 2006.
5. Ibid.
6. Abu Osama, "The Plague of the West," *Islambase.info*, http://islambase.info/index.php?option=com_content&task=view&id=32&Itemid=227 (accessed January 15, 2007).
7. Ibid.
8. Ibid.
9. Ibid.
10. The Saved Sect, "Homosexuality Today, Paedophilia Tomorrow," www.savioursect.co.uk (accessed January 14, 2006; site now discontinued).

11. Abu Osama, "The Plague of the West."
12. The Saved Sect, "Democracy=Terrorism," www.saviour sect.co.uk (accessed on January 14, 2006; site now discontinued).
13. Ibid.
14. Ali Bekhan, "Western Society: A Culture of paganism And disbelief," *Kavkaz Center.com*, December 1, 2006, http://kavkazcenter.com/eng/content/2006/12/01/6648.shtml (accessed 20, 2006 on http://www.millatibrahim.com [site now discontinued]).
15. Ibid.
16. Ibid.
17. Ibid.
18. Ibid.
19. The Saved Sect, "The Rotten Fruits of Democracy," www.savioursect.co.uk (accessed January 14, 2006; site now discontinued).
20. Ibid.
21. Ibid.
22. The Saved Sect, "The Ruling on Jihad and Its Divisions," www.savioursect.co.uk (accessed November 26, 2006; site now discontinued).
23. Al-Ghurabaa, "The Permissibility of Self-Sacrifice Operations," www.alghurabaa.co.uk (accessed October 17, 2005; site now discontinued).
24. Ibid.
25. Ibid.
26. Ibid.
27. Masood Azhar, "Virtues of Jihaad," *Bhatkallys.com*, http://www.bhatkallys.com/article/article.asp?aid=476 (accessed February 10, 2007).
28. Ibid.
29. Ibid.
30. Ibid.
31. "Jannah—The Ignored Puzzle Pieces of Knowledge," *Inshallahshaheed.com*, http://inshallahshaheed.wordpress.com/ (accessed February 10, 2006; site now discontinued).
32. The Ruling on the Jihad E-Book ,Yusuf al-Uraayi, www.saviorsect.co.uk, Date of publication unknown (accessed November 25, 2006).

Chapter 5: Online Training Videos

1. Al-Ghurabaa, Bosnia jihadi video, www.alghurabaa.co.uk (site now discontinued).
2. Ibid.

3. Ibid.
4. Ibid.
5. Ibid.
6. Yaakov Lappin, "Sweden threatened with jihad," *Ynetnews.com*, September 1, 2005,http://www.ynet.co.il/english/articles/0,7340,L-3135697,00.html(accessed January 9, 2005).
7. Ibid.
8. Top Ten Jihad video, circulated on several jihadi websites, (accessed February 8, 2005).
9. Ibid.
10. Ibid.
11. Ibid.

Chapter 6: The Online Weapons Factory and the Virtual Training Camp

1. Al-Firdaws, www.alfirdaws.org (accessed April 19, 2007; site now discontinued).
2. Ibid.
3. Ibid.
4. Ibid.
5. Ibid.
6. Ibid.
7. Ibid.
8. Ibid.
9. Ibid.
10. Ibid.
11. Ibid.
12. Abdul Hameed Bakier, "The New Issue of Technical Mujahid, a Training Manual for Jihadis," *Terrorism Monitor* 5, no. 6 (March 30, 2007), http://www.jamestown.org/single/?no_cache=1&tx_ttnews%5Bswords%5D=8fd5893941d69d0be3f378576261ae3e&tx_ttnews%5Bexact_search%5D=the%20new%20issue&tx_ttnews%5Btt_news%5D=1057&tx_ttnews%5BbackPid%5D=7&cHash=79ed95d817 (accessed May 30, 2007).
13. Ibid.
14. Ibid.
15. Ibid.
16. Alamuae, http://alamuae.com/vb/forumdisplay.php%3Ff%3D24&sa=X&oi=smap&resnum=1&ct=result&cd=2&usg=AFQjCNHCl7nsgyGSN-Jbc1L-hxkUD3qKK4g (accessed May 30, 2007).

17. Ibid.
18. Ibid.
19. Ibid.
20. Ibid.
21. Ibid.
22. Ibid.
23. Mojahid Mouslim, "Manual for Muslim Mujahid," http://mojahidmouslim.blogspot.com/ (accessed April 15, 2007).
24. Ibid.
25. Ibid.
26. Ibid.
27. Ibid.
28. Ibid.
29. Ibid.
30. Alamuae.
31. Ibid.
32. Ibid.
33. Ibid.
34. Ibid.
35. Ibid.
36. "'Police have crystal clear video image of car bomber,'" *The Daily Mail*, June 30, 2007, http://www.dailymail.co.uk/news/article-465068/Police-crystal-clear-video-image-car-bomber.html#ixzz0rm99K75b.
37. Chris Greenwood, "London Glasgow terrorist attacks: the men in the dock," *The Independent*, December 16, 2008, http://www.independent.co.uk/news/uk/crime/london-glasgow-terrorist-attacks-the-men-in-the-dock-1152513.html.

Chapter 7: The Ministry of Foreign Affairs

1. Omar Brooks, "covenant of a Muslim living among infidels," Muntadaa Forum (accessed November 20, 2006; site now discontinued), http://Muntadaaa.aswj.net.
2. Ibid.
3. Ibid.
4. Ibid.
5. Ibid.
6. Ibid.
7. Ibid.
8. Ibid.

9. Ibid.
10. Ibid.
11. Ibid.
12. Ibid.
13. Ibid.
14. Ibid.
15. Ibid.
16. Ibid.
17. Yaakov Lappin, "Al-Qaeda's Car Bomb Guide," *Ynetnews*, July 1, 2007.
18. "Bomb 'to split Spain from allies,'" *CNN.com*, March 16, 2004, http://edition.cnn.com (accessed June 26, 2007).
19. Global Research, "Madrid 'blueprint': a dodgy document," April 1, 2004, http://www.globalresearch.ca/articles/ONE404A.html (accessed June 20, 2010).
20. Bloomberg, "Zapatero's Iraq Pullout Pledge Raises Debate Over `Appeasement,'" April 1, 2004, http://www.bloomberg.com/apps/news?pid=newsarchive&sid=aOIH_qI3kVmM&refer=germany-redirectoldpage (accessed June 20, 2010).
21. Reuters, "Al-Qaeda group calls truce in Spain," *Sydney Morning Herald*, March 18, 2004, http://www.smh.com.au/articles/2004/03/18/1079199323371.html (accessed June 26, 2007).
22. AFP, "Al-Qaeda offers US troops month's truce to quit Iraq," *Breitbart*, December 22, 2005, http://www.breitbart.com/article.php?id=061222194627.k5dtw3l5&show_article=1 (accessed June 28, 2007).
23. Ibid.
24. Mohammed Al Shafey, "Al-Qaeda Reveals its Latest Threat: Rakan bin Williams," *Asharq Alawsat*, August 11, 2005, http://aawsat.com/english/news.asp?section=1&id=2577, (accessed June 22, 2007).
25. Ibid.
26. Ibid.
27. Ibid.
28. Jeffrey Anderson, "The Wild Goat Farmer," *LA Weekly*, September 15, 2005, http://www.laweekly.com/2005-09-15/news/the-wild-goat-farmer.
29. Ibid.
30. Al Shafey, "Al Qaeda Reveals . . . ."
31. Yaakov Lappin, "Jihadis aspire to 'conquer France,'" *Ynetnews.com*, April 23, 2007, http://www.ynetnews.com/articles/0,7340,L-3390982,00.html.
32. Ibid.
33. Ibid.

34. Ibid.
35. MEMRI, "Muslim Brotherhood Children's Website," *Special Dispatch* no. 1141 (April 18, 2006), http://www.memri.org/report/en/0/0/0/0/0/0/1663.htm.
36. Ibid.
37. Al-Ghurabaa, "Jihad For Palestine," www.alghurabaa.co.uk (accessed January 29, 2007; site now discontinued).
38. Ibid.
39. Islamic Awakening, "Stories of the martyrs of Chechnya," *Azzam Publications* 422, http://www.islamicawakening.com/viewarticle.php?articleID=422 (accessed July 1, 2007).
40. Ibid.
41. Ibid.
42. Jihaad Against Terrorism, http://al-jihaad.blogspot.com/ (accessed July 1, 2007).
43. Islamic-World.Net, "Our sympathy message for our dear brothers and sisters," http://www.Islamic-world.net (accessed February 20, 2007).

Chapter 8: Uploading the Virtual Caliphate

1. Al-Firdaws, forum on Hamas, www.alfirdaws.org (accessed June 28, 2007; site now discontinued). This post appeared under a subsection of the Firdaws forum dedicated to discussions by members on Hamas.
2. Imarat Islami of Afghanistan, http://www.alemarah.org/english.htm (accessed November 20, 2006; site now discontinued). The Imarat Islamic website posted a statement on its front page declaring that an Islamic emirate had been declared in Afghanistan.
3. Ibid.
4. Ibid.
5. "'Azzam the American' releases video focusing on Pakistan," *CNN.com/asia*, October 4, 2008, http://edition.cnn.com/2008/WORLD/asiapcf/10/04/gadahn.video/.
6. Ibid.
7. Al-Firdaws, "Appeal to Sunnis in Iraq," www.alfirdaws.org, December 18, 2006 (accessed July 2, 2007; site now discontinued).
8. Caliphate Voice Channel, http://cvc-online.blogspot.com/ (accessed July 2, 2007).
9. Ibid.
10. Ibid.
11. Al-Firdaws, Appeal to Sunnis in Iraq.
12. Ibid.

13. Al-Hanein, Islamic State statement, http://alhenein.com (accessed July 3, 2007).
14. Ibid.
15. Ibid.
16. Ibid.
17. Abu Baraa, "rise against the rulers" sermon, Paltalk chatroom, October 18, 2006.
18. Ibid.
19. Ibid.
20. Ibid.
21. Ibid.
22. The Saved Sect, statement on the Respect Party, www.savedsect.com (accessed August 30, 2005; site now discontinued).
23. Ibid.
24. Ibid.
25. Ibid.
26. Ibid.
27. Ibid.
28. Ibid.
29. Ibid.
30. Ibid.
31. Ibid.
32. Al-Ghurabaa, "How Islam Will Dominate the World," www.alghurabaa.co.uk (accessed February 4, 2006; site now discontinued).
33. Ibid.
34. Ibid.
35. Ibid.
36. Ibid.
37. Ibid.
38. Ibid.
39. Ibid.
40. Ibid.

Chapter 9: The Ministry of Morality

1. Abu Mizaan, online sermon on education, Paltalk chatroom, January 26, 2006.
2. Ibid.
3. Ibid.
4. Ibid.
5. History of Islam in the UK, *BBC*, September 9, 2009, http://www.bbc.co.uk/religion/religions/islam/history/uk_1.shtml.

6. Abu Mizaan, online sermon on education.
7. Ibid.
8. Ibid.
9. Ibid.
10. Ibid.
11. Ibid.
12. The Saved Sect, "Christian Crusade Against Islam Across Europe," http://web.archive.org/web/20060218104356/thesavedsect.com/articles/PressRelease/DemonstrationDanishEmbassy.htm (accessed July 19, 2007).
13. Ibid.
14. Ibid.
15. Ibid.
16. Ibid.
17. Owen Bowcott, "Arrest extremist marchers, police told," *The Guardian*, February 6, 2006, http://www.guardian.co.uk/uk/2006/feb/06/raceandreligion.muhammadcartoons.
18. The Saved Sect, "Christian Crusade."
19. Ibid.
20. Ibid.
21. Ibid.
22. Charlotte Gill, "Veiled protests as race-hate Muslims are jailed," *Daily Mail*, July 19, 2007, http://www.dailymail.co.uk/pages/live/articles/news/news.html?in_article_id=469285&in_page_id=1770&ito=newsnow.
23. Al-Ghurabaa, "Women and Jihad," www.alghurabaa.co.uk (site now discontinued).
24. Ibid.
25. Vikram Dodd, "Suicide bomber's family 'kept plan secret,'" *The Guardian*, April 27, 2004, http://www.guardian.co.uk/terrorism/story/0,12780,1204263,00.html (accessed July 25, 2007).
26. Ibid.
27. Sean O'Neill, "Bomber's wife 'is linked to radicals,'" *Times* (London), April 29, 2004, http://www.timesonline.co.uk (accessed July 25, 2007).
28. Paltalk.
29. Ibid.
30. "What role can sisters play in the jihad?" IslamicAwakening.com, http://www.islamicawakening.com/print.php?articleID=623 (accessed July 25, 2007).
31. "Islamic terrorists seeking to recruit women: report," *Daily Times*, March 5, 2005, http://www.dailytimes.com.pk/default.asp?page=story_5-3-2005_pg7_53 (accessed July 25, 2007).

32. "Naseehat for young wives," *The Majlis.net*, http://themajlis.net/Sections-article82-p1.html (accessed July 25, 2007).
33. Ibid.
34. Ibid.
35. Ibid.
36. Ibid.
37. Ibid.

Chapter 10: The Ministry of Finance

1. Mufti Khubiab Sahib, *Essential Provisions for the Mujahid*, http://www.alqimmah.net/showthread.php?t=17285 (Accessed June 20, 2010).
2. Ibid.
3. Ibid.
4. Ibid.
5. Ibid.
6. Ibid.
7. Ibid.
8. Ibid.
9. Ibid.
10. Ibid.
11. Ibid.
12. Ibid.
13. Ibid.
14. Aaron Weisburd, e-mail message to author, July 26, 2007.
15. Ibid.
16. Ibid.
17. Ibid.
18. Ibid.
19. "Only the Khilafah can make Poverty History," *Khilafah.com*, August 21, 2007, http://www.khilafah.com/index.php/the-khilafah/economy/842-only-the-khilafah-can-make-poverty-history (accessed September 26, 2007).
20. Ibid.
21. Ibid.
22. Ibid.
23. Ibid.
24. Ibid.
25. Ibid.

26. Ibid.
27. Ibid.
28. Ibid.
29. Ibid.
30. Ibid.
31. Ibid.
32. Ibid.

Chapter 11: Electronic Warfare

1. iReport, "Online Terror + Hate: The First Decade," Simon Wiesenthal Center, http://www.kintera.org/site/apps/s/link.asp?c=fwLYKnN8LzH&b=4145951 (accessed October 16, 2008).
2. Larry Greenemeier, "'Electronic Jihad' App Offers Cyberterrorism For The Masses," *Information Week*, July 2, 2007, http://www.informationweek.com/news/showArticle.jhtml?articleID=200001943 (accessed July 2, 2007).
3. Ibid.
4. Ibid.
5. John Stith, "New Danish Website Hacked," *Security Pro News*, February 14, 2006, http://www.securitypronews.com/news/securitynews/spn-45-20060214NewDanishWebsiteHacked.html.
6. Michelle Malkin, "The Islamists' War On The Internet," February 15, 2006, http://michellemalkin.com/2006/02/15/the-islamists-war-on-the-internet/.
7. Ibid.
8. Ibid. Users' e-mail addresses have been deleted.
9. Stephen Ulph, "Internet Mujahideen Refine Electronic Warfare Tactics," *Terrorism Focus* 3, no. 5 (February 7, 2006), http://www.jamestown.org/programs/gta/single/?tx_ttnews%5Btt_news%5D=666&tx_ttnews%5BbackPid%5D=239&no_cache=1.
10. Hacking Video, undated, www.alfirdaws.org (site discontinued, accessed May 10, 2007).
11. Steve Emerson, e-mail message to author, October 15, 2008.
12. Presentation by Yuval Elovici (Security Informatics and Terrorism-Patrolling the Web Conference, Ben-Gurion University of the Negev, Be'er Sheva, Israel, June 4, 2007).
13. Ibid.
14. Ibid.
15. Ibid.

16. Ibid.
17. Ibid.
18. Ibid.

Chapter 12: Online Clashes with Shiites and Iran

1. Hamad Al-Majid, "Shiite Expansion in Egypt: A Red Line," *Asharq Alawsat*, September, 17, 2008, http://www.aawsat.com/english/news.asp?section=2&id=14082.
2. "Top Muslim cleric group back Qaradawi over Shi'ites," Reuters, October 18, 2008, http://www.reuters.com/article/idUSTRE49H1A120081018.
3. Yaakov Lappin, "Islamist Cleric Issues Iran Warning," *Ynetnews.com*, August 27, 2007, http://www.ynet.co.il/english/articles/0,7340,L-3442337,00.html.
4. Ibid.
5. Ibid.
6. Ibid.
7. Ibid.
8. Al-Firdaws, anti-Shiite guide, www.alfirdaws.org (accessed September 2, 2007; site now discontinued).
9. Ibid.
10. Ibid.
11. Ibid.
12. Ibid.
13. Ibid.
14. Ibid.
15. Ibid.
16. Ibid.
17. "In Defense of Sunni Doctrine" section, Muslm forum, http://www.muslm.net (accessed September 7, 2007).
18. Ibid.
19. Ibid.

Chapter 13: Global Responses to the Rise of the Virtual Caliphate

1. Rod Radlauer, face-to-face interview with author, September 10, 2007.
2. Ibid.
3. Ibid.
4. Ibid.
5. Ibid.

6. Ibid.
7. Ibid.
8. Ibid.
9. Ibid.
10. Evan F. Kohlmann, "The Real Online Terrorist Threat," *Foreign Affairs* (September/October 2006), http://www.foreignaffairs.org/20060901faessay85510/evan-f-kohlmann/the-real-online-terrorist-threat.html.
11. Ellen Knickmeyer, "Al-Qaeda Web Forums Abruptly Taken Offline," *Washington Post*, October 18, 2008, http://www.washingtonpost.com/wp-dyn/content/article/2008/10/17/AR2008101703367.html.
12. Ibid.
13. Steve Emerson, e-mail message to author, October 15, 2008.
14. Comments by Yigal Carmon at cyber jihad panel (ICT 7th International Conference, Herzliya, Israel, September 11, 2007).
15. Ibid.
16. Ibid.

Chapter 14: Can the Virtual Caliphate Be Defeated?

1. Maria Alvanou, e-mail message to author, September 17, 2007.
2. Ibid.
3. Ibid.
4. Ibid.
5. Ibid.
6. Vladimir Golubev, "Internet and Security," Computer Crime Research Center, April 30, 2004, http://www.crime-research.org/news/30.04.2004/237/.
7. Presentation by Mark Goldberg (Security Informatics and Terrorism—Patrolling the Web Conference, Ben-Gurion University of the Negev, Be'er Sheva, Israel, June 4, 2007).
8. Presentation by Uri Hanani (Security Informatics and Terrorism-Patrolling the Web Conference, Ben Gurion University of the Negev, Be'er Sheva, Israel, June 4, 2007).
9. Ibid.
10. Ibid.
11. M. Last, A. Markov, and A. Kandel, "Multi-Lingual Detection of Terrorist Content on the Web," (paper, Proceedings of the PAKDD'06 International Workshop on Intelligence and Security Informatics [WISI'06], Singapore, April 9, 2006; lecture notes, *Computer Science* 3917 [2006]: 16–20).

12. Y. Elovici, B. Shapira, M. Last, O. Zaafrany, M. Friedman, M. Schneider, A. Kandel, "Content-Based Detection of Terrorists Browsing the Web Using an Advance Terror Detection System (ATDS)," (paper, Proceedings of the IEEE International Conference on Intelligence and Security Informatics [IEEE ISI'05], Atlanta, Georgia, May 19–20, 2005; lecture notes, Computer Science *3496* [2005]: 244–245).
13. Ibid.
14. Ibid.
15. Ibid.
16. Ibid.
17. Ibid.
18. Ibid.

Chapter 15: The Gathering Counteroffensive

1. Yael Shahar, e-mail message to author, September 19, 2007.
2. Ibid.
3. Ibid.
4. Ibid.
5. Presentation by Yael Shahar (ICT International Counter-Terrorism Conference, Herzliya, Israel, September 11, 2008).
6. Ibid.
7. Ibid.
8. Ibid.
9. Ibid.
10. Ibid.
11. Ibid.
12. Presentation given by Dr. Katharina Von Knop (ICT International Counter-Terrorism Conference, Herzliya, Israel, September 11, 2008).
13. Ibid.
14. Ibid.
15. Presentation given by Prof. Gabriel Weimann (ICT International Counter-Terrorism Conference, Herzliya, Israel, September 11, 2007).
16. Ibid.
17. Ibid.
18. Ibid.
19. Jeffrey F. Addicott, "Chapter eight: Cyberterrorism," *Terrorism Law: Materials, Cases, and Comments, Fourth Edition* (Tuscon, AZ: Lawyers and Judges, 2007).
20. Ibid.

21. Ibid.
22. Ibid.
23. Ibid.
24. Ibid.
25. Ibid.

Chapter 16: The Virtual Caliphate's WMD Program

1. Yaakov Lappin, "Jihadis Aspire To 'Conquer France,'" *Ynetnews.com*, April 23, 2007, http://www.ynet.co.il/english/articles/0,7340,L-3390982,00.html.
2. Ibid.
3. Ibid.
4. Ibid.
5. Michael Perry, "Sydney Nuclear Terror Plot Target-Police," Reuters, November 14, 2005, http://www.washingtonpost.com/wp-dyn/content/article/2005/11/14/AR2005111400036.html.
6. "'Why We Fight America': Al-Qa'ida Spokesman Explains September 11 and Declares Intentions to Kill 4 Million Americans with Weapons of Mass Destruction," *MEMRI: Special Dispatch Series* no. 338, June 12, 2002, http://www.memri.org/bin/articles.cgi?ID=SP38802.
7. Ibid.
8. Will McCants, "Nasir al-Fahd's Ruling on WMD," *jihadica.com*, June 5, 2008, http://www.jihadica.com/nasir-al-fahds-ruling-on-wmd/.
9. MEMRI video clip #1778, "The Emir of the Pakistani Taliban Beitullah Mahsoud: Pakistan Should Use Its Nuclear Weapons to Challenge the Enemies; Five Percent of Fighters in Afghanistan Are Our Men," May 26, 2008, http://www.memritv.org/clip/en/1778.htm.
10. "Obama Warns About Potential of Nuclear Terrorism," *Voice of America*, April 13, 2010, http://www1.voanews.com/english/news/usa/President-Obama-Risk-of-Nuclear-Attack-Increased-90746819.html.
11. "The Weapons of Mass Destruction Use Judgement [*sic*] Against the Unbelievers," Jill St. Claire's HomelandSecurityUS.NET, http://www.homelandsecurityus.net/WMD/weapons_of_mass_destruction_use_.htm (accessed September 25, 2007).
12. "Contemporary Islamist Ideology Authorizing Genocidal Murder," *MEMRI: Special Report* no. 25, January 27, 2004, http://www.memri.org/report/en/0/0/0/0/0/0/1049.htm.
13. Ibid.

14. Ibid.
15. Ibid.
16. Ibid.
17. Ibid.
18. Ibid.
19. Ibid.
20. Ibid.
21. Robert Wesley, "Al-Qaeda's WMD Strategy After the U.S. Intervention in Afghanistan," *Terrorism Monitor* 3, no. 20 (2005), http://www.jamestown.org/single/?no_cache=1&tx_ttnews%5Btt_news%5D=590.
22. Ibid.
23. Ibid.
24. Jonathan Spyer, "The Al-Qa'ida Network and Weapons of Mass Destruction," *Middle East Review of International Affairs* 8, no. 3 (September 2004), http://meria.idc.ac.il/journal/2004/issue3/spyer.pdf.
25. "Jihadist Forum Member Advocates a Chemical Weapon Attack on the Washington Metro Subway System," SITE Institute, August 11, 2005, http://siteinstitute.org/.
26. Saad al-Matrafi, "Terrorist Website Drops Dirty Bomb," *Arab News*, March 11, 2005, http://archive.arabnews.com/?page=1&section=0&article=60255&d=11&m=3&y=2005.
27. Ibid.
28. Ibid.

Chapter 17: Future Scenarios

1. Anwar al-Awlaki, *Allah is Preparing us for Victory*, ed. Mujahid fe Sabeelillah, trans. Amatullah, http://www.salaattime.com/downloads/anwar/Lectures/Allah%20is%20preparing%20us%20for%20victory.pdf (accessed September 26, 2007).
2. Ibid.
3. Ibid.
4. Ibid.
5. Ibid.
6. Ibid.
7. Ibid.
8. Ibid.
9. Ibid.

10. Ibid.
11. Ibid.

Chapter 18: Virtual Statehood?

1. Abu Hamza al-Masri, "Allah's Governance on Earth," Abu Hamza al-Masri, *Islamic Thinkers*, http://www.islamicthinkers.com/index/files/books/aqeedah/Allahs%20Governance%20on%20Earth.pdf.
2. "Ramadan, Unity, and Need for the Khalifah," *Hizb ut-Tahrir* Britain, September 15, 2007, http://www.hizb.org.uk/hizb/resources/leaflets/ramadhan-unity-and-need-for-the-khilafah.html.
3. Ibid.
4. Ibid.
5. Sheikh Omar Bakri Muhammad, "The Road to Jannah," IslamBase UK, http://downloads.islambase.co.uk/ (accessed September 26, 2007; site now discontinued).

Selected Sources

Addicott, Jeffrey F. *Terrorism Law: Materials, Cases, and Comments, Fourth Edition.* Tuscon, AZ: Lawyers and Judges, 2007.

AFP. "Al-Qaeda offers US troops month's truce to quit Iraq." *Breitbart*, December, 22, 2005. http://www.breitbart.com/article.php?id=061222194627.k5dtw3l5&show_article=1.

"Airport car bomb footage revealed." BBC News, October 13, 2008. http://news.bbc.co.uk/2/hi/uk_news/7667553.stm.

Al-Ghurabaa. Online jihadi video. www.ghurabaa.co.uk (site now discontinued). An altered version of the video can be found at http://www.youtube.com/watch?v=TjzxYdbiLk4&feature=related (accessed July 28, 2008).

Al-Ghurabaa. "The Permissibility of Self Sacrifice Operations." www.ghurabaa.co.uk (site now discontinued).

Al-Majid, Hamad. "Shiite Expansion in Egypt: A Red Line." *Asharq Alawsat*, September, 17, 2008. http://www.asharqalawsat.com/english/news.asp?section=2&id=14082.

Al-Matrafi, Saad. "Terrorist Website Drops Dirty Bomb." *Arab News*, March 11, 2005. http://archive.arabnews.com/?page=1&section=0&article=60255&d=11&m=3&y=2005.

Al Shafey, Mohammed. "Al-Qaeda Reveals its Latest Threat: Rakan bin Williams." *Asharq Alawsat*, August 11, 2005. http://aawsat.com/english/news.asp?section=1&id=2577.

Azhar, Masood. "Virtues of Jihaad." *Bhatkallys.com.* http://www.bhatkallys.com/article/article.asp?aid=476.

Azzam, Abdullah. *Defense of the Muslim Lands: The First Obligation after Iman.*

Translated by Brothers in Ribatt. http://www.religioscope.com/info/doc/jihad/azzam_defence_2_intro.htm.

"'Azzam the American' releases video focusing on Pakistan." *CNN.com/asia*, October 4, 2008. http://edition.cnn.com/2008/WORLD/asiapcf/10/04/gadahn.video/.

Bakier, Abdul Hameed. "The New Issue of Technical Mujahid, a Training Manual for Jihadis." *Terrorism Monitor* 5, no. 6 (March 30, 2007).

http://www.jamestown.org/single/?no_cache=1&tx_ttnews%5Bswords%5D=8fd5893941d69d0be3f378576261ae3e&tx_ttnews%5Bexact_search%5D=the%20new%20issue&tx_ttnews%5Btt_news%5D=1057&tx_ttnews%5BbackPid%5D=7&cHash=79ed95d817.

Bekhan, Ali. "Western Society: A Culture of paganism And disbelief." *KavkazCenter.com*, December 1, 2006. http://kavkazcenter.com/eng/content/2006/12/01/6648.shtml.

"Bomb 'to split Spain from allies.'" *CNN.com*, March 16, 2006. http://edition.cnn.com/2004/WORLD/europe/03/15/spain.invest/index.html.

Bowcott, Owen. "Arrest extremist marchers, police told." *The Guardian*, February 6, 2006. http://www.guardianco.uk/uk/2006/feb/06/raceandreligion.muhammad-cartoons.

Bunt, Gary R. Islam in the Digital Age: E-Jihad (London: Pluto Press, 2003)

Caliphate Voice Channel, http://cvc-online.blogspot.com/.

Dodd, Vikram. "Suicide bomber's family 'kept plan secret.'" *The Guardian*, April 27, 2004. http://www.guardian.co.uk/terrorism/story/0,12780,1204263,00.html.

Elovici, Y., B. Shapira, M. Last, O. Zaafrany, M. Friedman, M. Schneider, A. Kandel. "Content-Based Detection of Terrorists Browsing the Web Using an Advance Terror Detection System (ATDS)." (paper, Proceedings of the IEEE International Conference on Intelligence and Security Informatics [IEEE ISI'05], Atlanta, Georgia, May 19–20, 2005; lecture notes, Computer Science *3496* [2005]: 244–245).

Gill, Charlotte. "Veiled protests as race-hate Muslims are jailed." *Daily Mail*, July 19, 2007. http://www.dailymail.co.uk/pages/live/articles/news/news.html?in_article_id=469285&in_page_id=1770&ito=newsnow.

Greenemeier, Larry. "'Electronic Jihad' App Offers Cyberterrorism For The Masses." *Information Week*, July 2, 2007. http://www.informationweek.com/news/showArticle.jhtml?articleID=200001943.

Husain, Ed. *The Islamist: Why I Became an Islamic Fundamentalist, What I Saw Inside, and Why I Left*. London: Penguin Books, 2007.

"Jihadist Forum Member Advocates a Chemical Weapon Attack on the Washington

Metro Subway System." SITE Institute. August 11, 2005. http://siteinstitute.org/.

Imarat Islami of Afghanistan. http://www.alemarah.org/english.htm (site now discontinued).

iReport. "Online Terror + Hate: The First Decade." Simon Wiesenthal Center. http://www.kintera.org/site/apps/s/link.asp?c=fwLYKnN8LzH&b=4145951.

Islamic Awakening, "Stories of the martyrs of Chechnya," *Azzam Publications* 422. http://www.islamicawakening.com/viewarticle.php?articleID=422.

"Islamic terrorists seeking to recruit women: report." *Daily Mail*, March 5, 2005. http://www.dailytimes.com.pk/default.asp?page=story_5-3-2005_pg7_53.

Islamic Revival, http://www.khilafah.com/home/category_list.php?&category=Khilafah+Magazine&offset=0 (accessed May 16, 2006).

Knickmeyer, Ellen. "Al-Qaeda Web Forums Abruptly Taken Offline." *Washington Post*, October 18, 2008. http://www.washingtonpost.com/wp-dyn/content/article/2008/10/17/AR2008101703367.html.

Kohlmann, Evan F. "The Real Online Terrorist Threat." *Foreign Affairs* (September/October 2006). http://www.foreignaffairs.org/20060901faessay85510/evan-f-kohlmann/the-real-online-terrorist-threat.html.

Last, M., A. Markov, and A. Kandel. "Multi-Lingual Detection of Terrorist Content on the Web." (paper, Proceedings of the PAKDD'06 International Workshop on Intelligence and Security Informatics [WISI'06], Singapore, April 9, 2006; lecture notes, *Computer Science* 3917 [2006]: 16–20).

"Manual for Muslim Mujahid." Mojahid Mouslim. http://mojahidmouslim.blogspot.com/.

McCants, Will. "Nasir al-Fahd's Ruling on WMD." *jihadica.com*, June 5, 2008, http://www.jihadica.com/nasir-al-fahds-ruling-on-wmd/.

MEMRI. "Muslim Brotherhood Children's Website." *Special Dispatch* no. 1141 (April 18, 2006). http://www.memri.org/report/en/0/0/0/0/0/0/1663.htm.

Middle East Web. Osama Bin Laden—background and declaration of war. http://mideastweb.org/osamabinladen1.html.

Muhammad, Omar Bakri. "The Road to Jannah." IslamBase UK, http://downloads.islambase.co.uk/ (site now discontinued).

"Mujahideen Secrets." MEMRI Blog. http://www.thememriblog.org/blog_personal/en/239.htm.

"Naseehat for young wives." *The Majlis.net*, http://themajlis.net/Sections-article82-p1.html.

O'Neill, Sean. "Bomber's wife 'is linked to radicals.'" *Times* (London), April 29, 2004. http://www.timesonline.co.uk.

O'Neill, Sean, and Yaakov Lappin. "Extremist Islamist has returned – via internet." *Times* (London), February 26, 2006. http://www.timesonline.co.uk/tol/news/uk/article580990.ece (accessed October 21, 2005).

"Only the Khilafah can make Poverty History." *Khilafah.com*, August 21, 2007. http://www.khilafah.com/index.php/the-khilafah/economy/842-only-the-khilafah-can-make-poverty-history.

Osama, Abu. "The Plague of the West." *Islambase.info*. http://islambase.info/index.php?option=com_content&task=view&id=32&Itemid=227.

Perry, Michael. "Sydney Nuclear Terror Plot Target-Police." Reuters, November 14, 2005. http://www.washingtonpost.com/wp-dyn/content/article/2005/11/14/AR2005111400036.html.

Qutb, Sayyid. *Milestones*. http://majalla.org/books/2005/qutb-nilestone.pdf.

Reuters. "Al-Qaeda group calls truce in Spain." *Sydney Morning Herald*, March 18, 2004. http://www.smh.com.au/articles/2004/03/18/1079199323371.html.

Roy, Olivier. *Globalized Islam: The Search for a New Ummah*. New York: Columbia University Press, 2003.

Saved Sect, The. "Homosexuality Today, Paedophilia Tomorrow." www.savioursect.co.uk (site now discontinued).

Saved Sect, The. "The Rotten Fruits of Democracy." www.savioursect.co.uk (site now discontinued).

Saved Sect, The. "Christian Crusade Against Islam Across Europe, http://web.archive.org/web/20060218104356/thesavedsect.com/articles/PressRelease/DemonstrationDanishEmbassy.htm.

Saved Sect, The. "The Ruling on Jihad and Its Divisions." www.savioursect.co.uk (site now discontinued).

Spyer, Jonathan. "The Al-Qa'ida Network and Weapons of Mass Destruction." *Middle East Review of International Affairs* 8, no.3 (September 2004).

Stanley, Trevor. "Understanding the Origins of Wahhabism and Salafism." *Terrorism Monitor* 3, no. 14 (July 2005). http://www.jamestown.org/programs/gta/single/?tx_ttnews%5Btt_news%5D=528&tx_ttnews%5BbackPid%5D=180&no_cache=1.

Stemmann, Juan José Escobar. "Middle East Salafism's Influence and the Radicalization of Muslim Communities in Europe." *Middle East Review of International Affairs* 10, no. 3 (September 2006). http://meria.idc.ac.il/journal/2006/issue3/jv10no3a1.html#bio.

Stith, John. "New Danish Website Hacked." *Security Pro News*, February 14, 2006. http://www.securitypronews.com/news/securitynews/spn-45-20060214NewDanishWebsiteHacked.html.

"The growth of the virtual 'jihad' community," *ISN Security Watch*. http://www.isn.ethz.ch/ (site now discontinued).

Wesley, Robert. "Al-Qaeda's WMD Strategy After the U.S. Intervention in Afghanistan." *Terrorism Monitor* 3, no. 20 (2005). http://www.jamestown.org/single/?no_cache=1&tx_ttnews%5Btt_news%5D=590.

"What role can sisters play in the jihad?" *IslamicAwakening.com*. http://www.islamicawakening.com/print.php?articleID=623.

Index

About the Author

Yaakov Lappin is a journalist for the *Jerusalem Post,* where he covers the police, terrorism, and other security-related issues. His groundbreaking and exclusive coverage of jihadi activity on the Internet has appeared in the *London Times, Jerusalem Post*, and the English edition of Ynet, among other media outlets. A number of the author's reports for the *London Times* focused on an online declaration of war issued by notorious Islamist leaders in Britain six months before the July 7, 2005, London Underground bombings. He lives with his wife in Tel Aviv, Israel.